MW00790004

Totally Conceivable

Set In Soul

© 2019 Tatiana Media LLC in partnership with Set In Soul LLC

ISBN #: 978-1-949874-91-4

Published by Tatiana Media LLC

All rights reserved. No part of this journal/publication may be reproduced, stored in a retrieval system, or transmitted in any form or by any means, electronic, mechanical, photocopying, recording, scanning, or otherwise, except as permitted under Section 107 or 108 of the 1976 United States Copyright Act whatsoever without express written permission from the author, except in the case of brief quotations embodied in critical articles and reviews. Please refer all pertinent questions to the publisher.

Limit of Liability/Disclaimer of Warranty: While the publisher and author have used their best efforts in preparing this book/journal, they make no representations or warranties with respect to the accuracy or completeness of the contents of this book/journal and specifically disclaim any implied warranties. The advice and strategies contained herein may not be suitable for your situation. You should consult with a professional where appropriate. Neither the publisher nor author shall be liable for any loss of profit or any other emotional, physical, spiritual and mental distress and damages, including but not limited to special, incidental, consequential, or other damages.

For general information on our other products and services, please contact our Customer Support within the United States at support@setinsoul.com.

Tatiana Media LLC as well as Set In Soul LLC publishes its books in a variety of electronic formats. Some content that appears in print may not be available in electronic books.

This Journal Belongs To

_____

Dedicated To My Little Angel That Is
Coming. My Heart Is Excited.

Table Of Contents

How To Use This Journal

The ability to conceive is a very different experience for every woman. Every woman's body is different. We know how it feels to really try but feel like nothing seems to be happening. Stop your worrying and start putting your feelings down on paper. You know... the good, the bad and the truth. It is through writing you may discover what is preventing conception from happening right now or you may open yourself up to designing the kind of parent you want to be. This journal was created to help you trust the process. We believe your baby will be given to you when the time is right. For now get healthy and happy in mind, body and spirit.

Each night as you wind down, take the time to get to a place where you are present and mindful. It is then the daily prompts in this journal are to be filled out. These prompts address your thoughts and actions for the day as well as any changes within your body. By filling out the prompts each day, you will begin to see daily habits and thoughts that may or may not be helping you. This journal is to give you encouragement, as well as track your progress and put you in a place where you are not only building up your faith but also becoming a woman who just knows without a doubt that this will happen.

This journal is like having a best friend you can be honest with without any judgement. It is your companion through your journey to conceiving. This journal consists of different quotes of encouragement and affirmations. You can cut out the pages with the quotes and stick them to your wall to encourage you every day. The daily affirmations are there for you to repeat to yourself throughout the night and as you head to sleep. With this journal you release the pressures that you receive from family, friends and most importantly yourself. It's not about what anyone says. It's about what you believe and the actions that you take to support your beliefs. With this journal you can document your dreams, your prayer to conceive, your declaration statements and more.

It is not time for you to give up. Your baby will come at the right time. We just want you to believe that having a baby in your arms is totally conceivable.

About Me

About Me

Age: Birthdate:

I Live:

For A Living I Currently:

My Body Currently Feels:

What Makes Me Happy?

My Parents Are:

About Me

My Mother Had (Write Down How Many Children And Their Names):

How Many Children Did Each Of My Grandmothers Have?

How Many Children Do I Currently Have?

I Am Allergic To:

Have I Experienced Any Miscarriages?

About Me

My Partner Is:

My Current Family Consists Of:

I Currently Weigh:

My Period Length:

I Ovulate Approximately (List How Many Days After Your Period):

About Me

Current Health Complications I Have (Answer If Applicable):

How Am I Currently Working On My Health Complications
(Answer If Applicable)?

Foods I Love To Eat:

Foods I Avoid:

Foods That I Need To Avoid That I Love:

About Me

How Much Water Do I Currently Drink?

Do I Currently Consume Alcoholic Drinks?

Do I Smoke?

I Currently Exercise (Write How Often):

I Stay Active By:

About Me

I Currently Take These Supplements (Answer If Applicable):

I Sleep (Write Down How Many Hours):

How Often Do I Talk About Having Children?

How Often Do I Think About Not Being Pregnant Yet?

From One Through Ten With Ten Being The Highest, My Stress Level Is:

About Me

I Believe:

About My
Partner

About My Partner

Age: Birthdate:

My Partner Currently Makes A Living:

His Parents Are:

He Is Allergic To:

How Many Children Does My Partner Currently Have (Answer If Applicable)?

His Current Family Consist Of:

About My Partner

His Current Health Complications Are (Answer If Applicable):

How Is He Currently Working On His Health Complications (Answer If Applicable)?

Foods He Loves To Eat:

Foods He Avoids:

Foods That He Needs To Avoid That He Loves To Eat:

About My Partner

Foods He No Longer Avoids Now That We Are Trying To Conceive:

He Exercises (Write How Often):

He Currently Stays Active By:

He Currently Take These Supplements (Answer If Applicable):

He Currently Sleeps (Write Down How Many Hours):

About My Partner

Does He Drink?

Does He Smoke?

He Believes:

About My Child

About My Child

If My Child Is A Boy, His Name Will Be (Write The Name And The Meaning):

If My Child Is A Girl, Her Name Will Be (Write The Name And The Meaning):

About My Child

My Child Is:

My Child Loves:

My Child Feels:

My Child Laughs At:

My Child's Personality:

About My Child

My Child Looks Like:

My Child Smiles At:

My Child Eats:

What My Doctor Says

What My Doctor Says

How Many Doctors Have I Seen Since I First Started Trying To Conceive?

What Do I Look For In A Doctor?

My Doctor Is:

What Do I Like About My Doctor?

How Did I Find My Doctor?

What My Doctor Says

My Doctor Told Me:

My Doctor Said My Health Is:

My Doctor Said My Partner's Health Is (Answer If Applicable):

My Doctor Thinks:

My Doctor's Advice On Conceiving:

What My Doctor Says

Other Doctors I Have Consulted With About Conceiving:

What Have Other Doctors Advised Me About Conceiving And My
Chances of Conceiving (Answer If Applicable)?

What I Was Told I Need To Start Doing:

What My God Says

What My God Says

What Does God Say About Me?

What Do I Believe God Can Do?

What Do I Believe Is Already Done?

I Trust:

Because Of God:

What My God Says

What Does My God Say About My Baby?

God's Word Towards My Life:

What Does God Say About My Family?

My Trying To Conceive Prayer

My Trying To Conceive Prayer....

Dreams

Dreams I Have Had About Getting Pregnant And/Or Having A Child ....

Dreams Others Have Had About Me Getting Pregnant And/Or Having A Child ....

I Declare

I Declare....

The Start Of My Journey

The Start Of My Journey

How Long Have I Been Trying To Conceive?

I Believe Trying To Conceive Is:

I Started Trying To Conceive When:

Who Else Do I Know That Is Trying To Conceive?

Challenges We Have Faced Since Trying To Conceive:

The Start Of My Journey

Trying To Conceive Makes Me Feel:

Trying To Conceive Makes My Partner Feel:

We Try To Conceive (Write Down How Many Times A Week):

Things I Have Been Told To Do When Trying To Conceive:

How Many Children Do I Want?

The Start Of My Journey

In The Past, Having My Child/Children (Answer If Applicable):

I Noticed I Have Been:

I Am Preparing For Parenthood By:

What Is Causing Me Stress?

It Is Really Hard For Me:

The Start Of My Journey

Each Month:

It Is Not Easy To Predict:

I Ask God:

It Is Hard To Deal With:

Pregnancy Tests Make Me Feel:

The Start Of My Journey

False Alarms Make Me Feel:

In The Past, I Believed I Was Pregnant Because (Answer If Applicable):

Based On My Response To The Previous Prompt, When I Found Out
I Was Not Pregnant I Felt (Answer If Applicable):

In The Past, I Have Had To Go Through:

When I Have Tried To Conceive In The Past:

The Start Of My Journey

I Am Sensitive About:

What Do I Think Is Affecting Me From Getting Pregnant?

What Will I Do If Pregnancy Does Not Happen On Its Own?

This Process Is Emotional Because:

My Partner And I Are Willing To Try (Write For How Long):

The Start Of My Journey

Trying To Conceive Setbacks:

Close Friends I Can Talk To:

The Support I Get From My Family:

The Support I Get From My Friends:

The Support I Get From My Church:

The Start Of My Journey

When I Hear About Other Women Trying To Conceive, I Feel:

When I Hear About Other Women Getting Pregnant, I Feel:

I Do Not Want To Hear:

I Believe Ovulation Tests:

I Stopped Getting My Hopes Up Towards:

The Start Of My Journey

I Started Getting My Hopes Up Towards:

I Notice:

I Am Now More Aware:

Being Pregnant Means:

I Truly Feel:

The Start Of My Journey

I Never Told Anyone:

I Never Thought:

Having Sex Feels:

I Am Deciding:

My New Mindset On Trying To Get Pregnant:

The Start Of My Journey

I Cried When I Heard:

In The Past, We Have Tried:

I Am Upset That My Partner (Answer If Applicable):

I Have Always Been Told:

I Noticed My Body Changing By:

The Start Of My Journey

I Will Surround Myself With:

I Will Be Consistent With:

Some Things That I Believe Needs To Change:

I Will No Longer Allow Myself To Feel:

Trying To Conceive After A Miscarriage Feels (Answer If Applicable):

The Start Of My Journey

What I Am Keeping Between Me And God:

I Feel Good Knowing:

Because I Believe _____

I Will _____.

Creating In Love

Creating In Love

Date: Mood: Days Till Ovulation:

I Started My Day Believing: Last Night I Slept:

My Body Is: Did I Attempt To Conceive Last Night Or Anytime Today?

Today God Told Me: The Position I Attempted To Conceive In:

Today I Envisioned Myself: Did I Orgasm?

Today's Milestone: Basal Body Temperature:

Today I Ate: Cevical Mucus Changes:

Medications And Supplements I Took Today: Emotional Changes I Have Noticed Within Myself:

Did I Take A Pregnancy Test Today? Highlight Yes Or No.

If Yes, What Were The Results? _____.

I Am Blessed To Be Creating This Life Inside Of Me.

Creating In Love

I Am Letting My Faith Shape My Future.

Date: Mood: Days Till Ovulation:

I Started My Day Believing: Last Night I Slept:

My Body Is: Did I Attempt To Conceive Last Night Or Anytime Today?

Today God Told Me: The Position I Attempted To Conceive In:

Today I Envisioned Myself: Did I Orgasm?

Today's Milestone: Basal Body Temperature:

Today I Ate: Cevical Mucus Changes:

Medications And Supplements I Took Today: Emotional Changes I Have Noticed Within Myself:

Did I Take A Pregnancy Test Today? Highlight Yes Or No.

If Yes, What Were The Results? _____.

I Am Believing Great Things Are Happening For Me.

Creating In Love

Date: Mood: Days Till Ovulation:

I Started My Day Believing: Last Night I Slept:

My Body Is: Did I Attempt To Conceive Last Night
                                     Or Anytime Today?

Today God Told Me: The Position I Attempted To
                                     Conceive In:

Today I Envisioned Myself: Did I Orgasm?

Today's Milestone: Basal Body Temperature:

Today I Ate: Cevical Mucus Changes:

Medications And Supplements I Took   Emotional Changes I Have Noticed
Today: Within Myself:

Did I Take A Pregnancy Test Today? Highlight Yes Or No.

If Yes, What Were The Results? _____.

Faith Without Works Is Dead.

Creating In Love

Date: Mood: Days Till Ovulation:

I Started My Day Believing:	Last Night I Slept:
My Body Is:	Did I Attempt To Conceive Last Night Or Anytime Today?
Today God Told Me:	The Position I Attempted To Conceive In:
Today I Envisioned Myself:	Did I Orgasm?
Today's Milestone:	Basal Body Temperature:
Today I Ate:	Cevical Mucus Changes:
Medications And Supplements I Took Today:	Emotional Changes I Have Noticed Within Myself:

Did I Take A Pregnancy Test Today? Highlight Yes Or No.

If Yes, What Were The Results? _____.

Creating In Love

Date: Mood: Days Till Ovulation:

I Started My Day Believing: Last Night I Slept:

My Body Is: Did I Attempt To Conceive Last Night Or Anytime Today?

Today God Told Me: The Position I Attempted To Conceive In:

Today I Envisioned Myself: Did I Orgasm?

Today's Milestone: Basal Body Temperature:

Today I Ate: Cevical Mucus Changes:

Medications And Supplements I Took Today: Emotional Changes I Have Noticed Within Myself:

Did I Take A Pregnancy Test Today? Highlight Yes Or No.

If Yes, What Were The Results? _____.

My Personal Thoughts

When I Have My Baby, I Will Tell My Former Conceiving Self....

Creating In Love

Date: Mood: Days Till Ovulation:

I Started My Day Believing: Last Night I Slept:

My Body Is: Did I Attempt To Conceive Last Night Or Anytime Today?

Today God Told Me: The Position I Attempted To Conceive In:

Today I Envisioned Myself: Did I Orgasm?

Today's Milestone: Basal Body Temperature:

Today I Ate: Cevical Mucus Changes:

Medications And Supplements I Took Today: Emotional Changes I Have Noticed Within Myself:

Did I Take A Pregnancy Test Today? Highlight Yes Or No.

If Yes, What Were The Results? _____.

I Am Full Of Love For My Yet Unborn Child.

Creating In Love

Date: Mood: Days Till Ovulation:

I Started My Day Believing: Last Night I Slept:

My Body Is: Did I Attempt To Conceive Last Night Or Anytime Today?

Today God Told Me: The Position I Attempted To Conceive In:

Today I Envisioned Myself: Did I Orgasm?

Today's Milestone: Basal Body Temperature:

Today I Ate: Cevical Mucus Changes:

Medications And Supplements I Took Today: Emotional Changes I Have Noticed Within Myself:

Did I Take A Pregnancy Test Today? Highlight Yes Or No.

If Yes, What Were The Results? _____.

Creating In Love

Date: Mood: Days Till Ovulation:

I Started My Day Believing: Last Night I Slept:

My Body Is: Did I Attempt To Conceive Last Night
                                     Or Anytime Today?

Today God Told Me: The Position I Attempted To
                                     Conceive In:

Today I Envisioned Myself: Did I Orgasm?

Today's Milestone: Basal Body Temperature:

Today I Ate: Cevical Mucus Changes:

Medications And Supplements I Took   Emotional Changes I Have Noticed
Today: Within Myself:

Did I Take A Pregnancy Test Today? Highlight Yes Or No.

If Yes, What Were The Results? _____.

I Am Super Fertile.

I Will Be A Mommy.

Creating In Love

Date: Mood: Days Till Ovulation:

I Started My Day Believing: Last Night I Slept:

My Body Is: Did I Attempt To Conceive Last Night Or Anytime Today?

Today God Told Me: The Position I Attempted To Conceive In:

Today I Envisioned Myself: Did I Orgasm?

Today's Milestone: Basal Body Temperature:

Today I Ate: Cevical Mucus Changes:

Medications And Supplements I Took Today: Emotional Changes I Have Noticed Within Myself:

Did I Take A Pregnancy Test Today? Highlight Yes Or No.

If Yes, What Were The Results? _____.

Creating In Love

Date: Mood: Days Till Ovulation:

I Started My Day Believing: Last Night I Slept:

My Body Is: Did I Attempt To Conceive Last Night Or Anytime Today?

Today God Told Me: The Position I Attempted To Conceive In:

Today I Envisioned Myself: Did I Orgasm?

Today's Milestone: Basal Body Temperature:

Today I Ate: Cevical Mucus Changes:

Medications And Supplements I Took Today: Emotional Changes I Have Noticed Within Myself:

Did I Take A Pregnancy Test Today? Highlight Yes Or No.

If Yes, What Were The Results? _____.

Creating In Love

I Started My Day Believing: Last Night I Slept:

My Body Is: Did I Attempt To Conceive Last Night Or Anytime Today?

Today God Told Me: The Position I Attempted To Conceive In:

Today I Envisioned Myself: Did I Orgasm?

Today's Milestone: Basal Body Temperature:

Today I Ate: Cevical Mucus Changes:

Medications And Supplements I Took Today: Emotional Changes I Have Noticed Within Myself:

Did I Take A Pregnancy Test Today? Highlight Yes Or No.

If Yes, What Were The Results? _____.

My Body Is Designed To Conceive.

Creating In Love

Date: Mood: Days Till Ovulation:

I Started My Day Believing: Last Night I Slept:

My Body Is: Did I Attempt To Conceive Last Night Or Anytime Today?

Today God Told Me: The Position I Attempted To Conceive In:

Today I Envisioned Myself: Did I Orgasm?

Today's Milestone: Basal Body Temperature:

Today I Ate: Cevical Mucus Changes:

Medications And Supplements I Took Today: Emotional Changes I Have Noticed Within Myself:

Did I Take A Pregnancy Test Today? Highlight Yes Or No.

If Yes, What Were The Results? _____.

I Will Not Entertain Any Fears From Myself Or Others.

I Do Not Worry About It. I Pray About It.

Baby, You Are Worth Waiting For.

Creating In Love

Date: Mood: Days Till Ovulation:

I Started My Day Believing: Last Night I Slept:

My Body Is: Did I Attempt To Conceive Last Night
                                         Or Anytime Today?

Today God Told Me: The Position I Attempted To
                                         Conceive In:

Today I Envisioned Myself: Did I Orgasm?

Today's Milestone: Basal Body Temperature:

Today I Ate: Cevical Mucus Changes:

Medications And Supplements I Took   Emotional Changes I Have Noticed
Today: Within Myself:

Did I Take A Pregnancy Test Today? Highlight Yes Or No.

If Yes, What Were The Results? _____.

Creating In Love

Date: _____   Mood: _____   Days Till Ovulation: _____

I Started My Day Believing: | Last Night I Slept:

My Body Is: | Did I Attempt To Conceive Last Night
                                         | Or Anytime Today?

Today God Told Me: | The Position I Attempted To
                                         | Conceive In:

Today I Envisioned Myself: | Did I Orgasm?

Today's Milestone: | Basal Body Temperature:

Today I Ate: | Cevical Mucus Changes:

Medications And Supplements I Took | Emotional Changes I Have Noticed
Today: | Within Myself:

Did I Take A Pregnancy Test Today? Highlight Yes Or No.

If Yes, What Were The Results? _____.

I Have No Problems In Conceiving A Baby.

My Personal Thoughts

Creating In Love

Date: Mood: Days Till Ovulation:

I Started My Day Believing: Last Night I Slept:

My Body Is: Did I Attempt To Conceive Last Night
                                         Or Anytime Today?

Today God Told Me: The Position I Attempted To
                                         Conceive In:

Today I Envisioned Myself: Did I Orgasm?

Today's Milestone: Basal Body Temperature:

Today I Ate: Cevical Mucus Changes:

Medications And Supplements I Took   Emotional Changes I Have Noticed
Today: Within Myself:

Did I Take A Pregnancy Test Today? Highlight Yes Or No.

If Yes, What Were The Results? _____.

Creating In Love

Date: Mood: Days Till Ovulation:

I Started My Day Believing: Last Night I Slept:

My Body Is: Did I Attempt To Conceive Last Night
                                        Or Anytime Today?

Today God Told Me: The Position I Attempted To
                                        Conceive In:

Today I Envisioned Myself: Did I Orgasm?

Today's Milestone: Basal Body Temperature:

Today I Ate: Cevical Mucus Changes:

Medications And Supplements I Took   Emotional Changes I Have Noticed
Today: Within Myself:

Did I Take A Pregnancy Test Today? Highlight Yes Or No.

If Yes, What Were The Results? _____.

Creating In Love

Date: Mood: Days Till Ovulation:

I Started My Day Believing: Last Night I Slept:

My Body Is: Did I Attempt To Conceive Last Night Or Anytime Today?

Today God Told Me: The Position I Attempted To Conceive In:

Today I Envisioned Myself: Did I Orgasm?

Today's Milestone: Basal Body Temperature:

Today I Ate: Cevical Mucus Changes:

Medications And Supplements I Took Today: Emotional Changes I Have Noticed Within Myself:

Did I Take A Pregnancy Test Today? Highlight Yes Or No.

If Yes, What Were The Results? _____.

My Uterus Is In Perfect Condition.

Creating In Love

Date: Mood: Days Till Ovulation:

I Started My Day Believing: Last Night I Slept:

My Body Is: Did I Attempt To Conceive Last Night
                                         Or Anytime Today?

Today God Told Me: The Position I Attempted To
                                         Conceive In:

Today I Envisioned Myself: Did I Orgasm?

Today's Milestone: Basal Body Temperature:

Today I Ate: Cevical Mucus Changes:

Medications And Supplements I Took   Emotional Changes I Have Noticed
Today: Within Myself:

Did I Take A Pregnancy Test Today? Highlight Yes Or No.

If Yes, What Were The Results? _____.

The Best Part About Trying To Conceive....

I Pray For My Future Baby.

Creating In Love

Date: Mood: Days Till Ovulation:

I Started My Day Believing: Last Night I Slept:

My Body Is: Did I Attempt To Conceive Last Night Or Anytime Today?

Today God Told Me: The Position I Attempted To Conceive In:

Today I Envisioned Myself: Did I Orgasm?

Today's Milestone: Basal Body Temperature:

Today I Ate: Cevical Mucus Changes:

Medications And Supplements I Took Today: Emotional Changes I Have Noticed Within Myself:

Did I Take A Pregnancy Test Today? Highlight Yes Or No.

If Yes, What Were The Results? _____.

Creating In Love

Date: Mood: Days Till Ovulation:

I Started My Day Believing: Last Night I Slept:

My Body Is: Did I Attempt To Conceive Last Night
                                                   Or Anytime Today?

Today God Told Me: The Position I Attempted To
                                                   Conceive In:

Today I Envisioned Myself: Did I Orgasm?

Today's Milestone: Basal Body Temperature:

Today I Ate: Cevical Mucus Changes:

Medications And Supplements I Took   Emotional Changes I Have Noticed
Today: Within Myself:

Did I Take A Pregnancy Test Today? Highlight Yes Or No.

If Yes, What Were The Results? _____.

Creating In Love

Date: Mood: Days Till Ovulation:

I Started My Day Believing: Last Night I Slept:

My Body Is: Did I Attempt To Conceive Last Night
                                     Or Anytime Today?

Today God Told Me: The Position I Attempted To
                                     Conceive In:

Today I Envisioned Myself: Did I Orgasm?

Today's Milestone: Basal Body Temperature:

Today I Ate: Cevical Mucus Changes:

Medications And Supplements I Took   Emotional Changes I Have Noticed
Today: Within Myself:

Did I Take A Pregnancy Test Today? Highlight Yes Or No.

If Yes, What Were The Results? _____.

My Personal Thoughts

Once I Am Pregnant, I Will....

Creating In Love

I Am So Happy And Fortunate That God Has A Baby Ready For Me To Love Who Looks Just Like Me.

Date: Mood: Days Till Ovulation:

I Started My Day Believing:	Last Night I Slept:
My Body Is:	Did I Attempt To Conceive Last Night Or Anytime Today?
Today God Told Me:	The Position I Attempted To Conceive In:
Today I Envisioned Myself:	Did I Orgasm?
Today's Milestone:	Basal Body Temperature:
Today I Ate:	Cevical Mucus Changes:
Medications And Supplements I Took Today:	Emotional Changes I Have Noticed Within Myself:

Did I Take A Pregnancy Test Today? Highlight Yes Or No.

If Yes, What Were The Results? _____.

Creating In Love

Date: Mood: Days Till Ovulation:

I Started My Day Believing: Last Night I Slept:

My Body Is: Did I Attempt To Conceive Last Night Or Anytime Today?

Today God Told Me: The Position I Attempted To Conceive In:

Today I Envisioned Myself: Did I Orgasm?

Today's Milestone: Basal Body Temperature:

Today I Ate: Cevical Mucus Changes:

Medications And Supplements I Took Today: Emotional Changes I Have Noticed Within Myself:

Did I Take A Pregnancy Test Today? Highlight Yes Or No.

If Yes, What Were The Results? _____.

Each Day I Am Becoming More Fertile.

The First Few People I Will Tell Once I Am Pregnant....

Creating In Love

Date: Mood: Days Till Ovulation:

I Started My Day Believing: Last Night I Slept:

My Body Is: Did I Attempt To Conceive Last Night Or Anytime Today?

Today God Told Me: The Position I Attempted To Conceive In:

Today I Envisioned Myself: Did I Orgasm?

Today's Milestone: Basal Body Temperature:

Today I Ate: Cevical Mucus Changes:

Medications And Supplements I Took Today: Emotional Changes I Have Noticed Within Myself:

Did I Take A Pregnancy Test Today? Highlight Yes Or No.

If Yes, What Were The Results? _____.

Creating In Love

Date: Mood: Days Till Ovulation:

I Started My Day Believing: Last Night I Slept:

My Body Is: Did I Attempt To Conceive Last Night Or Anytime Today?

Today God Told Me: The Position I Attempted To Conceive In:

Today I Envisioned Myself: Did I Orgasm?

Today's Milestone: Basal Body Temperature:

Today I Ate: Cevical Mucus Changes:

Medications And Supplements I Took Today: Emotional Changes I Have Noticed Within Myself:

Did I Take A Pregnancy Test Today? Highlight Yes Or No.

If Yes, What Were The Results? _____.

Creating In Love

Date: Mood: Days Till Ovulation:

I Started My Day Believing: Last Night I Slept:

My Body Is: Did I Attempt To Conceive Last Night
                                     Or Anytime Today?

Today God Told Me: The Position I Attempted To
                                     Conceive In:

Today I Envisioned Myself: Did I Orgasm?

Today's Milestone: Basal Body Temperature:

Today I Ate: Cevical Mucus Changes:

Medications And Supplements I Took   Emotional Changes I Have Noticed
Today: Within Myself:

Did I Take A Pregnancy Test Today? Highlight Yes Or No.

If Yes, What Were The Results? _____.

I Am Releasing All My Fears And Worries About Time And Age.

91

My Personal Thoughts

Creating In Love

Date: Mood: Days Till Ovulation:

I Started My Day Believing: Last Night I Slept:

My Body Is: Did I Attempt To Conceive Last Night Or Anytime Today?

Today God Told Me: The Position I Attempted To Conceive In:

Today I Envisioned Myself: Did I Orgasm?

Today's Milestone: Basal Body Temperature:

Today I Ate: Cevical Mucus Changes:

Medications And Supplements I Took Today: Emotional Changes I Have Noticed Within Myself:

Did I Take A Pregnancy Test Today? Highlight Yes Or No.

If Yes, What Were The Results? _____.

Creating In Love

Date: Mood: Days Till Ovulation:

I Started My Day Believing:

Last Night I Slept:

My Body Is:

Did I Attempt To Conceive Last Night Or Anytime Today?

Today God Told Me:

The Position I Attempted To Conceive In:

Today I Envisioned Myself:

Did I Orgasm?

Today's Milestone:

Basal Body Temperature:

Today I Ate:

Cevical Mucus Changes:

Medications And Supplements I Took Today:

Emotional Changes I Have Noticed Within Myself:

Did I Take A Pregnancy Test Today? Highlight Yes Or No.

If Yes, What Were The Results? _____.

Creating In Love

Date: Mood: Days Till Ovulation:

I Started My Day Believing: Last Night I Slept:

My Body Is: Did I Attempt To Conceive Last Night Or Anytime Today?

Today God Told Me: The Position I Attempted To Conceive In:

Today I Envisioned Myself: Did I Orgasm?

Today's Milestone: Basal Body Temperature:

Today I Ate: Cevical Mucus Changes:

Medications And Supplements I Took Today: Emotional Changes I Have Noticed Within Myself:

Did I Take A Pregnancy Test Today? Highlight Yes Or No.

If Yes, What Were The Results? _____.

My Womb Is The Perfect Home For My Baby For The Next Few Months.

I Will Not Stress Over What I Expect To Happen.

You Are Already In My Heart.

Creating In Love

Date: Mood: Days Till Ovulation:

I Started My Day Believing: Last Night I Slept:

My Body Is: Did I Attempt To Conceive Last Night
                                                       Or Anytime Today?

Today God Told Me: The Position I Attempted To
                                                       Conceive In:

Today I Envisioned Myself: Did I Orgasm?

Today's Milestone: Basal Body Temperature:

Today I Ate: Cevical Mucus Changes:

Medications And Supplements I Took   Emotional Changes I Have Noticed
Today: Within Myself:

Did I Take A Pregnancy Test Today? Highlight Yes Or No.

If Yes, What Were The Results? _____.

Creating In Love

Date: _____ Mood: _____ Days Till Ovulation: _____

I Started My Day Believing:

Last Night I Slept:

My Body Is:

Did I Attempt To Conceive Last Night Or Anytime Today?

Today God Told Me:

The Position I Attempted To Conceive In:

Today I Envisioned Myself:

Did I Orgasm?

Today's Milestone:

Basal Body Temperature:

Today I Ate:

Cevical Mucus Changes:

Medications And Supplements I Took Today:

Emotional Changes I Have Noticed Within Myself:

Did I Take A Pregnancy Test Today? Highlight Yes Or No.

If Yes, What Were The Results? _____.

I Direct Positive Energy Towards My Reproductive System.

Creating In Love

I Am A Healthy, Strong, And Very Fertile Woman.

Date: Mood: Days Till Ovulation:

I Started My Day Believing: Last Night I Slept:

My Body Is: Did I Attempt To Conceive Last Night Or Anytime Today?

Today God Told Me: The Position I Attempted To Conceive In:

Today I Envisioned Myself: Did I Orgasm?

Today's Milestone: Basal Body Temperature:

Today I Ate: Cevical Mucus Changes:

Medications And Supplements I Took Today: Emotional Changes I Have Noticed Within Myself:

Did I Take A Pregnancy Test Today? Highlight Yes Or No.

If Yes, What Were The Results? _____.

I Predict That My Pregnancy Will....

Creating In Love

Date: Mood: Days Till Ovulation:

I Started My Day Believing: Last Night I Slept:

My Body Is: Did I Attempt To Conceive Last Night Or Anytime Today?

Today God Told Me: The Position I Attempted To Conceive In:

Today I Envisioned Myself: Did I Orgasm?

Today's Milestone: Basal Body Temperature:

Today I Ate: Cevical Mucus Changes:

Medications And Supplements I Took Today: Emotional Changes I Have Noticed Within Myself:

Did I Take A Pregnancy Test Today? Highlight Yes Or No.

If Yes, What Were The Results? _____.

Creating In Love

Date: Mood: Days Till Ovulation:

I Started My Day Believing: Last Night I Slept:

My Body Is: Did I Attempt To Conceive Last Night Or Anytime Today?

Today God Told Me: The Position I Attempted To Conceive In:

Today I Envisioned Myself: Did I Orgasm?

Today's Milestone: Basal Body Temperature:

Today I Ate: Cevical Mucus Changes:

Medications And Supplements I Took Today: Emotional Changes I Have Noticed Within Myself:

Did I Take A Pregnancy Test Today? Highlight Yes Or No.

If Yes, What Were The Results? _____.

Creating In Love

Date: Mood: Days Till Ovulation:

I Started My Day Believing: Last Night I Slept:

My Body Is: Did I Attempt To Conceive Last Night Or Anytime Today?

Today God Told Me: The Position I Attempted To Conceive In:

Today I Envisioned Myself: Did I Orgasm?

Today's Milestone: Basal Body Temperature:

Today I Ate: Cevical Mucus Changes:

Medications And Supplements I Took Today: Emotional Changes I Have Noticed Within Myself:

Did I Take A Pregnancy Test Today? Highlight Yes Or No.

If Yes, What Were The Results? _____.

Everyday I Am One Day Closer To Conceiving.

Creating In Love

Date: Mood: Days Till Ovulation:

I Started My Day Believing: Last Night I Slept:

My Body Is: Did I Attempt To Conceive Last Night
                                     Or Anytime Today?

Today God Told Me: The Position I Attempted To
                                     Conceive In:

Today I Envisioned Myself: Did I Orgasm?

Today's Milestone: Basal Body Temperature:

Today I Ate: Cevical Mucus Changes:

Medications And Supplements I Took   Emotional Changes I Have Noticed
Today: Within Myself:

Did I Take A Pregnancy Test Today? Highlight Yes Or No.

If Yes, What Were The Results? _____.

My Body Is Getting To Be More Relaxed Each Day.

Creating In Love

Date: Mood: Days Till Ovulation:

I Started My Day Believing: Last Night I Slept:

My Body Is: Did I Attempt To Conceive Last Night Or Anytime Today?

Today God Told Me: The Position I Attempted To Conceive In:

Today I Envisioned Myself: Did I Orgasm?

Today's Milestone: Basal Body Temperature:

Today I Ate: Cevical Mucus Changes:

Medications And Supplements I Took Today: Emotional Changes I Have Noticed Within Myself:

Did I Take A Pregnancy Test Today? Highlight Yes Or No.

If Yes, What Were The Results? _____.

It Is Very Easy For Me To Release Tension And Stress.

My Personal Thoughts

Creating In Love

Date: Mood: Days Till Ovulation:

I Started My Day Believing: Last Night I Slept:

My Body Is: Did I Attempt To Conceive Last Night
                                         Or Anytime Today?

Today God Told Me: The Position I Attempted To
                                         Conceive In:

Today I Envisioned Myself: Did I Orgasm?

Today's Milestone: Basal Body Temperature:

Today I Ate: Cevical Mucus Changes:

Medications And Supplements I Took   Emotional Changes I Have Noticed
Today: Within Myself:

Did I Take A Pregnancy Test Today? Highlight Yes Or No.

If Yes, What Were The Results? _____.

I Enjoy Creating Life Out Of Love.

Creating In Love

Date: Mood: Days Till Ovulation:

I Started My Day Believing: Last Night I Slept:

My Body Is: Did I Attempt To Conceive Last Night Or Anytime Today?

Today God Told Me: The Position I Attempted To Conceive In:

Today I Envisioned Myself: Did I Orgasm?

Today's Milestone: Basal Body Temperature:

Today I Ate: Cevical Mucus Changes:

Medications And Supplements I Took Today: Emotional Changes I Have Noticed Within Myself:

Did I Take A Pregnancy Test Today? Highlight Yes Or No.

If Yes, What Were The Results? _____.

Creating In Love

Date: Mood: Days Till Ovulation:

I Started My Day Believing: Last Night I Slept:

My Body Is: Did I Attempt To Conceive Last Night Or Anytime Today?

Today God Told Me: The Position I Attempted To Conceive In:

Today I Envisioned Myself: Did I Orgasm?

Today's Milestone: Basal Body Temperature:

Today I Ate: Cevical Mucus Changes:

Medications And Supplements I Took Today: Emotional Changes I Have Noticed Within Myself:

Did I Take A Pregnancy Test Today? Highlight Yes Or No.

If Yes, What Were The Results? _____.

Creating In Love

Date: Mood: Days Till Ovulation:

I Started My Day Believing: Last Night I Slept:

My Body Is: Did I Attempt To Conceive Last Night Or Anytime Today?

Today God Told Me: The Position I Attempted To Conceive In:

Today I Envisioned Myself: Did I Orgasm?

Today's Milestone: Basal Body Temperature:

Today I Ate: Cevical Mucus Changes:

Medications And Supplements I Took Today: Emotional Changes I Have Noticed Within Myself:

Did I Take A Pregnancy Test Today? Highlight Yes Or No.

If Yes, What Were The Results? _____.

Even Miracles Take A Little Time.

As Soon As I Decided To Try To Conceive, I Also Decided To Change....

Creating In Love

Date: Mood: Days Till Ovulation:

I Started My Day Believing: Last Night I Slept:

My Body Is: Did I Attempt To Conceive Last Night Or Anytime Today?

Today God Told Me: The Position I Attempted To Conceive In:

Today I Envisioned Myself: Did I Orgasm?

Today's Milestone: Basal Body Temperature:

Today I Ate: Cevical Mucus Changes:

Medications And Supplements I Took Today: Emotional Changes I Have Noticed Within Myself:

Did I Take A Pregnancy Test Today? Highlight Yes Or No.

If Yes, What Were The Results? _____.

I Release All The Unwanted Emotional Patterns That I Have Built Up Within Me.

115

Creating In Love

Date: Mood: Days Till Ovulation:

I Started My Day Believing: Last Night I Slept:

My Body Is: Did I Attempt To Conceive Last Night
                                               Or Anytime Today?

Today God Told Me: The Position I Attempted To
                                               Conceive In:

Today I Envisioned Myself: Did I Orgasm?

Today's Milestone: Basal Body Temperature:

Today I Ate: Cevical Mucus Changes:

Medications And Supplements I Took   Emotional Changes I Have Noticed
Today: Within Myself:

Did I Take A Pregnancy Test Today? Highlight Yes Or No.

If Yes, What Were The Results? _____.

Creating In Love

Date: Mood: Days Till Ovulation:

I Started My Day Believing: Last Night I Slept:

My Body Is: Did I Attempt To Conceive Last Night
                                     Or Anytime Today?

Today God Told Me: The Position I Attempted To
                                     Conceive In:

Today I Envisioned Myself: Did I Orgasm?

Today's Milestone: Basal Body Temperature:

Today I Ate: Cevical Mucus Changes:

Medications And Supplements I Took   Emotional Changes I Have Noticed
Today: Within Myself:

Did I Take A Pregnancy Test Today? Highlight Yes Or No.

If Yes, What Were The Results? _____.

I Will Stay In My Bubble Of Feeling Good And Believing In Good Things Happening. It Is In My Bubble Things Manifest.

Just Because It Did Not Happen Today Does Not Mean It Will Not Happen Tomorrow.

Creating In Love

Date: Mood: Days Till Ovulation:

I Started My Day Believing: Last Night I Slept:

My Body Is: Did I Attempt To Conceive Last Night Or Anytime Today?

Today God Told Me: The Position I Attempted To Conceive In:

Today I Envisioned Myself: Did I Orgasm?

Today's Milestone: Basal Body Temperature:

Today I Ate: Cevical Mucus Changes:

Medications And Supplements I Took Today: Emotional Changes I Have Noticed Within Myself:

Did I Take A Pregnancy Test Today? Highlight Yes Or No.

If Yes, What Were The Results? _____.

Creating In Love

Date: Mood: Days Till Ovulation:

I Started My Day Believing: Last Night I Slept:

My Body Is: Did I Attempt To Conceive Last Night
                                     Or Anytime Today?

Today God Told Me: The Position I Attempted To
                                     Conceive In:

Today I Envisioned Myself: Did I Orgasm?

Today's Milestone: Basal Body Temperature:

Today I Ate: Cevical Mucus Changes:

Medications And Supplements I Took   Emotional Changes I Have Noticed
Today: Within Myself:

Did I Take A Pregnancy Test Today? Highlight Yes Or No.

If Yes, What Were The Results? _____.

Creating In Love

Date: Mood: Days Till Ovulation:

I Started My Day Believing: Last Night I Slept:

My Body Is: Did I Attempt To Conceive Last Night
                                     Or Anytime Today?

Today God Told Me: The Position I Attempted To
                                     Conceive In:

Today I Envisioned Myself: Did I Orgasm?

Today's Milestone: Basal Body Temperature:

Today I Ate: Cevical Mucus Changes:

Medications And Supplements I Took   Emotional Changes I Have Noticed
Today: Within Myself:

Did I Take A Pregnancy Test Today? Highlight Yes Or No.

If Yes, What Were The Results? _____.

My Personal Thoughts

Creating In Love

Date: Mood: Days Till Ovulation:

I Started My Day Believing: Last Night I Slept:

My Body Is: Did I Attempt To Conceive Last Night Or Anytime Today?

Today God Told Me: The Position I Attempted To Conceive In:

Today I Envisioned Myself: Did I Orgasm?

Today's Milestone: Basal Body Temperature:

Today I Ate: Cevical Mucus Changes:

Medications And Supplements I Took Today: Emotional Changes I Have Noticed Within Myself:

Did I Take A Pregnancy Test Today? Highlight Yes Or No.

If Yes, What Were The Results? _____.

Creating In Love

Date: Mood: Days Till Ovulation:

I Started My Day Believing: Last Night I Slept:

My Body Is: Did I Attempt To Conceive Last Night Or Anytime Today?

Today God Told Me: The Position I Attempted To Conceive In:

Today I Envisioned Myself: Did I Orgasm?

Today's Milestone: Basal Body Temperature:

Today I Ate: Cevical Mucus Changes:

Medications And Supplements I Took Today: Emotional Changes I Have Noticed Within Myself:

Did I Take A Pregnancy Test Today? Highlight Yes Or No.

If Yes, What Were The Results? _____.

Creating In Love

Date: Mood: Days Till Ovulation:

I Started My Day Believing: Last Night I Slept:

My Body Is: Did I Attempt To Conceive Last Night Or Anytime Today?

Today God Told Me: The Position I Attempted To Conceive In:

Today I Envisioned Myself: Did I Orgasm?

Today's Milestone: Basal Body Temperature:

Today I Ate: Cevical Mucus Changes:

Medications And Supplements I Took Today: Emotional Changes I Have Noticed Within Myself:

Did I Take A Pregnancy Test Today? Highlight Yes Or No.

If Yes, What Were The Results? _____.

"Trust in the Lord with all your heart; do not depend on your own understanding. Seek his will in all you do, and he will direct your paths."

- Proverbs 3:5-6

Creating In Love

Date: Mood: Days Till Ovulation:

I Started My Day Believing: Last Night I Slept:

My Body Is: Did I Attempt To Conceive Last Night Or Anytime Today?

Today God Told Me: The Position I Attempted To Conceive In:

Today I Envisioned Myself: Did I Orgasm?

Today's Milestone: Basal Body Temperature:

Today I Ate: Cevical Mucus Changes:

Medications And Supplements I Took Today: Emotional Changes I Have Noticed Within Myself:

Did I Take A Pregnancy Test Today? Highlight Yes Or No.

If Yes, What Were The Results? _____.

Creating In Love

Date: Mood: Days Till Ovulation:

I Started My Day Believing: Last Night I Slept:

My Body Is: Did I Attempt To Conceive Last Night
                                     Or Anytime Today?

Today God Told Me: The Position I Attempted To
                                     Conceive In:

Today I Envisioned Myself: Did I Orgasm?

Today's Milestone: Basal Body Temperature:

Today I Ate: Cevical Mucus Changes:

Medications And Supplements I Took   Emotional Changes I Have Noticed
Today: Within Myself:

Did I Take A Pregnancy Test Today? Highlight Yes Or No.

If Yes, What Were The Results? _____.

I Always Visualize Having A Healthy Baby.

129

Creating In Love

Date: Mood: Days Till Ovulation:

I Started My Day Believing: Last Night I Slept:

My Body Is: Did I Attempt To Conceive Last Night
                                         Or Anytime Today?

Today God Told Me: The Position I Attempted To
                                         Conceive In:

Today I Envisioned Myself: Did I Orgasm?

Today's Milestone: Basal Body Temperature:

Today I Ate: Cevical Mucus Changes:

Medications And Supplements I Took   Emotional Changes I Have Noticed
Today: Within Myself:

Did I Take A Pregnancy Test Today? Highlight Yes Or No.

If Yes, What Were The Results? _____.

My Choices Reflect What I Expect.

Do not be anxious about anything, but in every situation, by prayer and petition, with thanksgiving, present your requests to God. And the peace of God, which transcends all understanding, will guard your hearts and your minds in Christ Jesus.

– Philippians 4:6-7

It Is A
Choice To Run
Out Of Hope.
I Am
Choosing To
Keep It.

Creating In Love

Date: Mood: Days Till Ovulation:

I Started My Day Believing: | Last Night I Slept:

My Body Is: | Did I Attempt To Conceive Last Night
                                     | Or Anytime Today?

Today God Told Me: | The Position I Attempted To
                                     | Conceive In:

Today I Envisioned Myself: | Did I Orgasm?

Today's Milestone: | Basal Body Temperature:

Today I Ate: | Cevical Mucus Changes:

Medications And Supplements I Took | Emotional Changes I Have Noticed
Today: | Within Myself:

Did I Take A Pregnancy Test Today? Highlight Yes Or No.

If Yes, What Were The Results? _____.

Creating In Love

Date: Mood: Days Till Ovulation:

I Started My Day Believing: Last Night I Slept:

My Body Is: Did I Attempt To Conceive Last Night Or Anytime Today?

Today God Told Me: The Position I Attempted To Conceive In:

Today I Envisioned Myself: Did I Orgasm?

Today's Milestone: Basal Body Temperature:

Today I Ate: Cevical Mucus Changes:

Medications And Supplements I Took Today: Emotional Changes I Have Noticed Within Myself:

Did I Take A Pregnancy Test Today? Highlight Yes Or No.

If Yes, What Were The Results? _____.

My Personal Thoughts

Creating In Love

Date: Mood: Days Till Ovulation:

I Started My Day Believing: Last Night I Slept:

My Body Is: Did I Attempt To Conceive Last Night Or Anytime Today?

Today God Told Me: The Position I Attempted To Conceive In:

Today I Envisioned Myself: Did I Orgasm?

Today's Milestone: Basal Body Temperature:

Today I Ate: Cevical Mucus Changes:

Medications And Supplements I Took Today: Emotional Changes I Have Noticed Within Myself:

Did I Take A Pregnancy Test Today? Highlight Yes Or No.

If Yes, What Were The Results? _____.

I Have Perfectly Balanced Hormones In My Body.

Creating In Love

Date: Mood: Days Till Ovulation:

I Started My Day Believing: Last Night I Slept:

My Body Is: Did I Attempt To Conceive Last Night
                                         Or Anytime Today?

Today God Told Me: The Position I Attempted To
                                         Conceive In:

Today I Envisioned Myself: Did I Orgasm?

Today's Milestone: Basal Body Temperature:

Today I Ate: Cevical Mucus Changes:

Medications And Supplements I Took   Emotional Changes I Have Noticed
Today: Within Myself:

Did I Take A Pregnancy Test Today? Highlight Yes Or No.

If Yes, What Were The Results? _____.

Creating In Love

Date: Mood: Days Till Ovulation:

I Started My Day Believing: Last Night I Slept:

My Body Is: Did I Attempt To Conceive Last Night Or Anytime Today?

Today God Told Me: The Position I Attempted To Conceive In:

Today I Envisioned Myself: Did I Orgasm?

Today's Milestone: Basal Body Temperature:

Today I Ate: Cevical Mucus Changes:

Medications And Supplements I Took Today: Emotional Changes I Have Noticed Within Myself:

Did I Take A Pregnancy Test Today? Highlight Yes Or No.

If Yes, What Were The Results? _____.

I Am Ready For New Life To Enter My Life.

Creating In Love

Date: Mood: Days Till Ovulation:

I Started My Day Believing: Last Night I Slept:

My Body Is: Did I Attempt To Conceive Last Night Or Anytime Today?

Today God Told Me: The Position I Attempted To Conceive In:

Today I Envisioned Myself: Did I Orgasm?

Today's Milestone: Basal Body Temperature:

Today I Ate: Cevical Mucus Changes:

Medications And Supplements I Took Today: Emotional Changes I Have Noticed Within Myself:

Did I Take A Pregnancy Test Today? Highlight Yes Or No.

If Yes, What Were The Results? _____.

I Am A Very Good Provider To My Newborn Child.

I Am Suppose To Grow Through This.

There Is
No Doubt
That This
Will
Happen
For Me.

Creating In Love

Date: Mood: Days Till Ovulation:

I Started My Day Believing: Last Night I Slept:

My Body Is: Did I Attempt To Conceive Last Night Or Anytime Today?

Today God Told Me: The Position I Attempted To Conceive In:

Today I Envisioned Myself: Did I Orgasm?

Today's Milestone: Basal Body Temperature:

Today I Ate: Cevical Mucus Changes:

Medications And Supplements I Took Today: Emotional Changes I Have Noticed Within Myself:

Did I Take A Pregnancy Test Today? Highlight Yes Or No.

If Yes, What Were The Results? _____.

Creating In Love

Date: Mood: Days Till Ovulation:

I Started My Day Believing: Last Night I Slept:

My Body Is: Did I Attempt To Conceive Last Night
                                         Or Anytime Today?

Today God Told Me: The Position I Attempted To
                                         Conceive In:

Today I Envisioned Myself: Did I Orgasm?

Today's Milestone: Basal Body Temperature:

Today I Ate: Cevical Mucus Changes:

Medications And Supplements I Took   Emotional Changes I Have Noticed
Today: Within Myself:

Did I Take A Pregnancy Test Today? Highlight Yes Or No.

If Yes, What Were The Results? _____.

Creating In Love

Date: Mood: Days Till Ovulation:

I Started My Day Believing: Last Night I Slept:

My Body Is: Did I Attempt To Conceive Last Night Or Anytime Today?

Today God Told Me: The Position I Attempted To Conceive In:

Today I Envisioned Myself: Did I Orgasm?

Today's Milestone: Basal Body Temperature:

Today I Ate: Cevical Mucus Changes:

Medications And Supplements I Took Today: Emotional Changes I Have Noticed Within Myself:

Did I Take A Pregnancy Test Today? Highlight Yes Or No.

If Yes, What Were The Results? _____.

Creating In Love

Date: Mood: Days Till Ovulation:

I Started My Day Believing: Last Night I Slept:

My Body Is: Did I Attempt To Conceive Last Night Or Anytime Today?

Today God Told Me: The Position I Attempted To Conceive In:

Today I Envisioned Myself: Did I Orgasm?

Today's Milestone: Basal Body Temperature:

Today I Ate: Cevical Mucus Changes:

Medications And Supplements I Took Today: Emotional Changes I Have Noticed Within Myself:

Did I Take A Pregnancy Test Today? Highlight Yes Or No.

If Yes, What Were The Results? _____.

146

Signs Of My Most Fertile Days....

I
Already
Heard
Yes.

"Therefore I tell you, whatever you ask for in prayer, believe that you have received it and it will be yours."

– Mark 11:24

Creating In Love

Date: Mood: Days Till Ovulation:

I Started My Day Believing: Last Night I Slept:

My Body Is: Did I Attempt To Conceive Last Night Or Anytime Today?

Today God Told Me: The Position I Attempted To Conceive In:

Today I Envisioned Myself: Did I Orgasm?

Today's Milestone: Basal Body Temperature:

Today I Ate: Cevical Mucus Changes:

Medications And Supplements I Took Today: Emotional Changes I Have Noticed Within Myself:

Did I Take A Pregnancy Test Today? Highlight Yes Or No.

If Yes, What Were The Results? _____.

Creating In Love

Date: Mood: Days Till Ovulation:

I Started My Day Believing: | Last Night I Slept:

My Body Is: | Did I Attempt To Conceive Last Night
                                     | Or Anytime Today?

Today God Told Me: | The Position I Attempted To
                                     | Conceive In:

Today I Envisioned Myself: | Did I Orgasm?

Today's Milestone: | Basal Body Temperature:

Today I Ate: | Cevical Mucus Changes:

Medications And Supplements I Took | Emotional Changes I Have Noticed
Today: | Within Myself:

Did I Take A Pregnancy Test Today? Highlight Yes Or No.

If Yes, What Were The Results? _____.

Creating In Love

Date: Mood: Days Till Ovulation:

I Started My Day Believing: | Last Night I Slept:

My Body Is: | Did I Attempt To Conceive Last Night Or Anytime Today?

Today God Told Me: | The Position I Attempted To Conceive In:

Today I Envisioned Myself: | Did I Orgasm?

Today's Milestone: | Basal Body Temperature:

Today I Ate: | Cevical Mucus Changes:

Medications And Supplements I Took Today: | Emotional Changes I Have Noticed Within Myself:

Did I Take A Pregnancy Test Today? Highlight Yes Or No.

If Yes, What Were The Results? _____.

Creating In Love

Date: Mood: Days Till Ovulation:

I Started My Day Believing: Last Night I Slept:

My Body Is: Did I Attempt To Conceive Last Night
                                     Or Anytime Today?

Today God Told Me: The Position I Attempted To
                                     Conceive In:

Today I Envisioned Myself: Did I Orgasm?

Today's Milestone: Basal Body Temperature:

Today I Ate: Cevical Mucus Changes:

Medications And Supplements I Took   Emotional Changes I Have Noticed
Today: Within Myself:

Did I Take A Pregnancy Test Today? Highlight Yes Or No.

If Yes, What Were The Results? _____.

I Declare Myself To Be Fertile And Healthy.

Soon Enough My Baby Will Look Me In My Face And Smile Right Back At Me.

I Do Not
Ask God
Why.
I Just Get
Ready.

Creating In Love

Date: Mood: Days Till Ovulation:

I Started My Day Believing: Last Night I Slept:

My Body Is: Did I Attempt To Conceive Last Night Or Anytime Today?

Today God Told Me: The Position I Attempted To Conceive In:

Today I Envisioned Myself: Did I Orgasm?

Today's Milestone: Basal Body Temperature:

Today I Ate: Cevical Mucus Changes:

Medications And Supplements I Took Today: Emotional Changes I Have Noticed Within Myself:

Did I Take A Pregnancy Test Today? Highlight Yes Or No.

If Yes, What Were The Results? _____.

Creating In Love

Date: Mood: Days Till Ovulation:

I Started My Day Believing: Last Night I Slept:

My Body Is: Did I Attempt To Conceive Last Night
                                     Or Anytime Today?

Today God Told Me: The Position I Attempted To
                                     Conceive In:

Today I Envisioned Myself: Did I Orgasm?

Today's Milestone: Basal Body Temperature:

Today I Ate: Cevical Mucus Changes:

Medications And Supplements I Took   Emotional Changes I Have Noticed
Today: Within Myself:

Did I Take A Pregnancy Test Today? Highlight Yes Or No.

If Yes, What Were The Results? _____.

My Personal Thoughts

Creating In Love

Date: Mood: Days Till Ovulation:

I Started My Day Believing: Last Night I Slept:

My Body Is: Did I Attempt To Conceive Last Night
                                                 Or Anytime Today?

Today God Told Me: The Position I Attempted To
                                                 Conceive In:

Today I Envisioned Myself: Did I Orgasm?

Today's Milestone: Basal Body Temperature:

Today I Ate: Cevical Mucus Changes:

Medications And Supplements I Took   Emotional Changes I Have Noticed
Today: Within Myself:

Did I Take A Pregnancy Test Today? Highlight Yes Or No.

If Yes, What Were The Results? _____.

Creating In Love

Date: Mood: Days Till Ovulation:

I Started My Day Believing: Last Night I Slept:

My Body Is: Did I Attempt To Conceive Last Night Or Anytime Today?

Today God Told Me: The Position I Attempted To Conceive In:

Today I Envisioned Myself: Did I Orgasm?

Today's Milestone: Basal Body Temperature:

Today I Ate: Cevical Mucus Changes:

Medications And Supplements I Took Today: Emotional Changes I Have Noticed Within Myself:

Did I Take A Pregnancy Test Today? Highlight Yes Or No.

If Yes, What Were The Results? _____.

Creating In Love

Date: Mood: Days Till Ovulation:

I Started My Day Believing:

Last Night I Slept:

My Body Is:

Did I Attempt To Conceive Last Night Or Anytime Today?

Today God Told Me:

The Position I Attempted To Conceive In:

Today I Envisioned Myself:

Did I Orgasm?

Today's Milestone:

Basal Body Temperature:

Today I Ate:

Cevical Mucus Changes:

Medications And Supplements I Took Today:

Emotional Changes I Have Noticed Within Myself:

Did I Take A Pregnancy Test Today? Highlight Yes Or No.

If Yes, What Were The Results? _____.

I Am Strong And Healthy In Mind, Body And Soul.

Creating In Love

Date: Mood: Days Till Ovulation:

I Started My Day Believing:	Last Night I Slept:
My Body Is:	Did I Attempt To Conceive Last Night Or Anytime Today?
Today God Told Me:	The Position I Attempted To Conceive In:
Today I Envisioned Myself:	Did I Orgasm?
Today's Milestone:	Basal Body Temperature:
Today I Ate:	Cevical Mucus Changes:
Medications And Supplements I Took Today:	Emotional Changes I Have Noticed Within Myself:

Did I Take A Pregnancy Test Today? Highlight Yes Or No.

If Yes, What Were The Results? _____.

I Am Now Surrendering To Nature's Power.

Even When It Is Dark I Look For The Stars.

Creating In Love

Date: Mood: Days Till Ovulation:

I Started My Day Believing: Last Night I Slept:

My Body Is: Did I Attempt To Conceive Last Night Or Anytime Today?

Today God Told Me: The Position I Attempted To Conceive In:

Today I Envisioned Myself: Did I Orgasm?

Today's Milestone: Basal Body Temperature:

Today I Ate: Cevical Mucus Changes:

Medications And Supplements I Took Today: Emotional Changes I Have Noticed Within Myself:

Did I Take A Pregnancy Test Today? Highlight Yes Or No.

If Yes, What Were The Results? _____.

Creating In Love

Date: Mood: Days Till Ovulation:

I Started My Day Believing: Last Night I Slept:

My Body Is: Did I Attempt To Conceive Last Night Or Anytime Today?

Today God Told Me: The Position I Attempted To Conceive In:

Today I Envisioned Myself: Did I Orgasm?

Today's Milestone: Basal Body Temperature:

Today I Ate: Cevical Mucus Changes:

Medications And Supplements I Took Today: Emotional Changes I Have Noticed Within Myself:

Did I Take A Pregnancy Test Today? Highlight Yes Or No.

If Yes, What Were The Results? _____.

I Release Everything That Blocks My Connection To My Inner Self.

Creating In Love

Date: Mood: Days Till Ovulation:

I Started My Day Believing:	Last Night I Slept:
My Body Is:	Did I Attempt To Conceive Last Night Or Anytime Today?
Today God Told Me:	The Position I Attempted To Conceive In:
Today I Envisioned Myself:	Did I Orgasm?
Today's Milestone:	Basal Body Temperature:
Today I Ate:	Cevical Mucus Changes:
Medications And Supplements I Took Today:	Emotional Changes I Have Noticed Within Myself:

Did I Take A Pregnancy Test Today? Highlight Yes Or No.

If Yes, What Were The Results? _____.

I Hope My Future Daughter/Son Is Able To....

Creating In Love

Date: Mood: Days Till Ovulation:

I Started My Day Believing: Last Night I Slept:

My Body Is: Did I Attempt To Conceive Last Night Or Anytime Today?

Today God Told Me: The Position I Attempted To Conceive In:

Today I Envisioned Myself: Did I Orgasm?

Today's Milestone: Basal Body Temperature:

Today I Ate: Cevical Mucus Changes:

Medications And Supplements I Took Today: Emotional Changes I Have Noticed Within Myself:

Did I Take A Pregnancy Test Today? Highlight Yes Or No.

If Yes, What Were The Results? _____.

Creating In Love

Date: Mood: Days Till Ovulation:

I Started My Day Believing: Last Night I Slept:

My Body Is: Did I Attempt To Conceive Last Night
                                     Or Anytime Today?

Today God Told Me: The Position I Attempted To
                                     Conceive In:

Today I Envisioned Myself: Did I Orgasm?

Today's Milestone: Basal Body Temperature:

Today I Ate: Cevical Mucus Changes:

Medications And Supplements I Took   Emotional Changes I Have Noticed
Today: Within Myself:

Did I Take A Pregnancy Test Today? Highlight Yes Or No.

If Yes, What Were The Results? _____.

I Am Creating A Healthy Space Externally And Internally For Myself And My Baby.

Soon Enough I Will Be Saying I Am Happy, Healthy And Pregnant.

Creating In Love

Date: Mood: Days Till Ovulation:

I Started My Day Believing: Last Night I Slept:

My Body Is: Did I Attempt To Conceive Last Night Or Anytime Today?

Today God Told Me: The Position I Attempted To Conceive In:

Today I Envisioned Myself: Did I Orgasm?

Today's Milestone: Basal Body Temperature:

Today I Ate: Cevical Mucus Changes:

Medications And Supplements I Took Today: Emotional Changes I Have Noticed Within Myself:

Did I Take A Pregnancy Test Today? Highlight Yes Or No.

If Yes, What Were The Results? _____.

Creating In Love

Date: Mood: Days Till Ovulation:

I Started My Day Believing: Last Night I Slept:

My Body Is: Did I Attempt To Conceive Last Night Or Anytime Today?

Today God Told Me: The Position I Attempted To Conceive In:

Today I Envisioned Myself: Did I Orgasm?

Today's Milestone: Basal Body Temperature:

Today I Ate: Cevical Mucus Changes:

Medications And Supplements I Took Today: Emotional Changes I Have Noticed Within Myself:

Did I Take A Pregnancy Test Today? Highlight Yes Or No.

If Yes, What Were The Results? _____.

I Am Capable Of Being A Loving And Caring Mother To My Child.

My Personal Thoughts

Creating In Love

Date: Mood: Days Till Ovulation:

I Started My Day Believing: Last Night I Slept:

My Body Is: Did I Attempt To Conceive Last Night Or Anytime Today?

Today God Told Me: The Position I Attempted To Conceive In:

Today I Envisioned Myself: Did I Orgasm?

Today's Milestone: Basal Body Temperature:

Today I Ate: Cevical Mucus Changes:

Medications And Supplements I Took Today: Emotional Changes I Have Noticed Within Myself:

Did I Take A Pregnancy Test Today? Highlight Yes Or No.

If Yes, What Were The Results? _____.

I Release All My Concerns And Fears About Infertility.

Creating In Love

Date: Mood: Days Till Ovulation:

I Started My Day Believing: Last Night I Slept:

My Body Is: Did I Attempt To Conceive Last Night Or Anytime Today?

Today God Told Me: The Position I Attempted To Conceive In:

Today I Envisioned Myself: Did I Orgasm?

Today's Milestone: Basal Body Temperature:

Today I Ate: Cevical Mucus Changes:

Medications And Supplements I Took Today: Emotional Changes I Have Noticed Within Myself:

Did I Take A Pregnancy Test Today? Highlight Yes Or No.

If Yes, What Were The Results? _____.

Creating In Love

Date: Mood: Days Till Ovulation:

I Started My Day Believing: Last Night I Slept:

My Body Is: Did I Attempt To Conceive Last Night
                                     Or Anytime Today?

Today God Told Me: The Position I Attempted To
                                     Conceive In:

Today I Envisioned Myself: Did I Orgasm?

Today's Milestone: Basal Body Temperature:

Today I Ate: Cevical Mucus Changes:

Medications And Supplements I Took   Emotional Changes I Have Noticed
Today: Within Myself:

Did I Take A Pregnancy Test Today? Highlight Yes Or No.

If Yes, What Were The Results? _____.

Creating In Love

Date: Mood: Days Till Ovulation:

I Started My Day Believing: | Last Night I Slept:

My Body Is: | Did I Attempt To Conceive Last Night Or Anytime Today?

Today God Told Me: | The Position I Attempted To Conceive In:

Today I Envisioned Myself: | Did I Orgasm?

Today's Milestone: | Basal Body Temperature:

Today I Ate: | Cevical Mucus Changes:

Medications And Supplements I Took Today: | Emotional Changes I Have Noticed Within Myself:

Did I Take A Pregnancy Test Today? Highlight Yes Or No.

If Yes, What Were The Results? _____.

The Best Trying To Conceive Advice I Have Received....

I Stopped Stressing Every Month And Started Expecting My Blessings.

Creating In Love

Date: Mood: Days Till Ovulation:

I Started My Day Believing: Last Night I Slept:

My Body Is: Did I Attempt To Conceive Last Night Or Anytime Today?

Today God Told Me: The Position I Attempted To Conceive In:

Today I Envisioned Myself: Did I Orgasm?

Today's Milestone: Basal Body Temperature:

Today I Ate: Cevical Mucus Changes:

Medications And Supplements I Took Today: Emotional Changes I Have Noticed Within Myself:

Did I Take A Pregnancy Test Today? Highlight Yes Or No.

If Yes, What Were The Results? _____.

I Always Eat Healthy Foods To Get My Body Ready To Conceive.

Creating In Love

Date: Mood: Days Till Ovulation:

I Started My Day Believing: Last Night I Slept:

My Body Is: Did I Attempt To Conceive Last Night Or Anytime Today?

Today God Told Me: The Position I Attempted To Conceive In:

Today I Envisioned Myself: Did I Orgasm?

Today's Milestone: Basal Body Temperature:

Today I Ate: Cevical Mucus Changes:

Medications And Supplements I Took Today: Emotional Changes I Have Noticed Within Myself:

Did I Take A Pregnancy Test Today? Highlight Yes Or No.

If Yes, What Were The Results? _____.

I Only Crave For Food That Will Improve My Wellbeing.

182

Creating In Love

Date: Mood: Days Till Ovulation:

I Started My Day Believing: Last Night I Slept:

My Body Is: Did I Attempt To Conceive Last Night Or Anytime Today?

Today God Told Me: The Position I Attempted To Conceive In:

Today I Envisioned Myself: Did I Orgasm?

Today's Milestone: Basal Body Temperature:

Today I Ate: Cevical Mucus Changes:

Medications And Supplements I Took Today: Emotional Changes I Have Noticed Within Myself:

Did I Take A Pregnancy Test Today? Highlight Yes Or No.

If Yes, What Were The Results? _____.

I Consume A Lot Of Fresh Vegetables And Fruits Each Day.

183

It Does Not
Matter How
Long It
Will Take,
I Will Stay
Prepared.

My
Blessings
Will Make
An Impact
In This
World.

Creating In Love

Date: Mood: Days Till Ovulation:

I Started My Day Believing: Last Night I Slept:

My Body Is: Did I Attempt To Conceive Last Night Or Anytime Today?

Today God Told Me: The Position I Attempted To Conceive In:

Today I Envisioned Myself: Did I Orgasm?

Today's Milestone: Basal Body Temperature:

Today I Ate: Cevical Mucus Changes:

Medications And Supplements I Took Today: Emotional Changes I Have Noticed Within Myself:

Did I Take A Pregnancy Test Today? Highlight Yes Or No.

If Yes, What Were The Results? _____.

Creating In Love

Date: Mood: Days Till Ovulation:

I Started My Day Believing: Last Night I Slept:

My Body Is: Did I Attempt To Conceive Last Night
                                                     Or Anytime Today?

Today God Told Me: The Position I Attempted To
                                                     Conceive In:

Today I Envisioned Myself: Did I Orgasm?

Today's Milestone: Basal Body Temperature:

Today I Ate: Cevical Mucus Changes:

Medications And Supplements I Took   Emotional Changes I Have Noticed
Today: Within Myself:

Did I Take A Pregnancy Test Today? Highlight Yes Or No.

If Yes, What Were The Results? _____.

My Pregnancy Will Be Amazing.

Creating In Love

Date: Mood: Days Till Ovulation:

I Started My Day Believing: Last Night I Slept:

My Body Is: Did I Attempt To Conceive Last Night
                                     Or Anytime Today?

Today God Told Me: The Position I Attempted To
                                     Conceive In:

Today I Envisioned Myself: Did I Orgasm?

Today's Milestone: Basal Body Temperature:

Today I Ate: Cevical Mucus Changes:

Medications And Supplements I Took   Emotional Changes I Have Noticed
Today: Within Myself:

Did I Take A Pregnancy Test Today? Highlight Yes Or No.

If Yes, What Were The Results? _____.

Creating In Love

Date: Mood: Days Till Ovulation:

I Started My Day Believing: Last Night I Slept:

My Body Is: Did I Attempt To Conceive Last Night Or Anytime Today?

Today God Told Me: The Position I Attempted To Conceive In:

Today I Envisioned Myself: Did I Orgasm?

Today's Milestone: Basal Body Temperature:

Today I Ate: Cevical Mucus Changes:

Medications And Supplements I Took Today: Emotional Changes I Have Noticed Within Myself:

Did I Take A Pregnancy Test Today? Highlight Yes Or No.

If Yes, What Were The Results? _____.

I Am Making Only Healthy Food Choices.

189

I Want God To Know....

Creating In Love

Date: Mood: Days Till Ovulation:

I Started My Day Believing: Last Night I Slept:

My Body Is: Did I Attempt To Conceive Last Night Or Anytime Today?

Today God Told Me: The Position I Attempted To Conceive In:

Today I Envisioned Myself: Did I Orgasm?

Today's Milestone: Basal Body Temperature:

Today I Ate: Cevical Mucus Changes:

Medications And Supplements I Took Today: Emotional Changes I Have Noticed Within Myself:

Did I Take A Pregnancy Test Today? Highlight Yes Or No.

If Yes, What Were The Results? _____.

My Pregnancy Feels Good. My Baby Feels Good Within Me.

191

Creating In Love

Date: Mood: Days Till Ovulation:

I Started My Day Believing: Last Night I Slept:

My Body Is: Did I Attempt To Conceive Last Night Or Anytime Today?

Today God Told Me: The Position I Attempted To Conceive In:

Today I Envisioned Myself: Did I Orgasm?

Today's Milestone: Basal Body Temperature:

Today I Ate: Cevical Mucus Changes:

Medications And Supplements I Took Today: Emotional Changes I Have Noticed Within Myself:

Did I Take A Pregnancy Test Today? Highlight Yes Or No.

If Yes, What Were The Results? _____.

Creating In Love

Date: Mood: Days Till Ovulation:

I Started My Day Believing: | Last Night I Slept:

My Body Is: | Did I Attempt To Conceive Last Night
                                     | Or Anytime Today?

Today God Told Me: | The Position I Attempted To
                                     | Conceive In:

Today I Envisioned Myself: | Did I Orgasm?

Today's Milestone: | Basal Body Temperature:

Today I Ate: | Cevical Mucus Changes:

Medications And Supplements I Took | Emotional Changes I Have Noticed
Today: | Within Myself:

Did I Take A Pregnancy Test Today? Highlight Yes Or No.

If Yes, What Were The Results? _____.

I Release What Is Keeping Me From Receiving What Is Ready For Me.

Creating In Love

I Am Feeling Safe And Truly Loved Right Now.

Date: Mood: Days Till Ovulation:

I Started My Day Believing: Last Night I Slept:

My Body Is: Did I Attempt To Conceive Last Night Or Anytime Today?

Today God Told Me: The Position I Attempted To Conceive In:

Today I Envisioned Myself: Did I Orgasm?

Today's Milestone: Basal Body Temperature:

Today I Ate: Cevical Mucus Changes:

Medications And Supplements I Took Today: Emotional Changes I Have Noticed Within Myself:

Did I Take A Pregnancy Test Today? Highlight Yes Or No.

If Yes, What Were The Results? _____.

It Is Going To Happen For Me.

Be joyful in hope, patient in affliction, faithful in prayer.

– Romans 12:12

Creating In Love

Date: Mood: Days Till Ovulation:

I Started My Day Believing: | Last Night I Slept:

My Body Is: | Did I Attempt To Conceive Last Night
                                     | Or Anytime Today?

Today God Told Me: | The Position I Attempted To
                                     | Conceive In:

Today I Envisioned Myself: | Did I Orgasm?

Today's Milestone: | Basal Body Temperature:

Today I Ate: | Cevical Mucus Changes:

Medications And Supplements I Took | Emotional Changes I Have Noticed
Today: | Within Myself:

Did I Take A Pregnancy Test Today? Highlight Yes Or No.

If Yes, What Were The Results? _____.

Creating In Love

Date: Mood: Days Till Ovulation:

I Started My Day Believing: Last Night I Slept:

My Body Is: Did I Attempt To Conceive Last Night Or Anytime Today?

Today God Told Me: The Position I Attempted To Conceive In:

Today I Envisioned Myself: Did I Orgasm?

Today's Milestone: Basal Body Temperature:

Today I Ate: Cevical Mucus Changes:

Medications And Supplements I Took Today: Emotional Changes I Have Noticed Within Myself:

Did I Take A Pregnancy Test Today? Highlight Yes Or No.

If Yes, What Were The Results? _____.

Creating In Love

Date: Mood: Days Till Ovulation:

I Started My Day Believing: Last Night I Slept:

My Body Is: Did I Attempt To Conceive Last Night
                                     Or Anytime Today?

Today God Told Me: The Position I Attempted To
                                     Conceive In:

Today I Envisioned Myself: Did I Orgasm?

Today's Milestone: Basal Body Temperature:

Today I Ate: Cevical Mucus Changes:

Medications And Supplements I Took   Emotional Changes I Have Noticed
Today: Within Myself:

Did I Take A Pregnancy Test Today? Highlight Yes Or No.

If Yes, What Were The Results? _____.

Creating In Love

Date: Mood: Days Till Ovulation:

I Started My Day Believing: | Last Night I Slept:

My Body Is: | Did I Attempt To Conceive Last Night
                                     | Or Anytime Today?

Today God Told Me: | The Position I Attempted To
                                     | Conceive In:

Today I Envisioned Myself: | Did I Orgasm?

Today's Milestone: | Basal Body Temperature:

Today I Ate: | Cevical Mucus Changes:

Medications And Supplements I Took | Emotional Changes I Have Noticed
Today: | Within Myself:

Did I Take A Pregnancy Test Today? Highlight Yes Or No.

If Yes, What Were The Results? _____.

My Personal Thoughts

My First Day As A Parent Will Be....

Creating In Love

Date: Mood: Days Till Ovulation:

I Started My Day Believing:

Last Night I Slept:

My Body Is:

Did I Attempt To Conceive Last Night Or Anytime Today?

Today God Told Me:

The Position I Attempted To Conceive In:

Today I Envisioned Myself:

Did I Orgasm?

Today's Milestone:

Basal Body Temperature:

Today I Ate:

Cevical Mucus Changes:

Medications And Supplements I Took Today:

Emotional Changes I Have Noticed Within Myself:

Did I Take A Pregnancy Test Today? Highlight Yes Or No.

If Yes, What Were The Results? _____.

Creating In Love

Date: Mood: Days Till Ovulation:

I Started My Day Believing: | Last Night I Slept:

My Body Is: | Did I Attempt To Conceive Last Night Or Anytime Today?

Today God Told Me: | The Position I Attempted To Conceive In:

Today I Envisioned Myself: | Did I Orgasm?

Today's Milestone: | Basal Body Temperature:

Today I Ate: | Cevical Mucus Changes:

Medications And Supplements I Took Today: | Emotional Changes I Have Noticed Within Myself:

Did I Take A Pregnancy Test Today? Highlight Yes Or No.

If Yes, What Were The Results? _____.

204

Creating In Love

Date: Mood: Days Till Ovulation:

I Started My Day Believing: Last Night I Slept:

My Body Is: Did I Attempt To Conceive Last Night
                                     Or Anytime Today?

Today God Told Me: The Position I Attempted To
                                     Conceive In:

Today I Envisioned Myself: Did I Orgasm?

Today's Milestone: Basal Body Temperature:

Today I Ate: Cevical Mucus Changes:

Medications And Supplements I Took   Emotional Changes I Have Noticed
Today: Within Myself:

Did I Take A Pregnancy Test Today? Highlight Yes Or No.

If Yes, What Were The Results? _____.

I Look Forward To The Changes Within My Body.

"By faith Abraham, even though he was past age—and Sarah herself was barren—was enabled to become a father because he considered him faithful who had made the promise. And so from this one man, and he as good as dead, came descendants as numerous as the stars in the sky and as countless as the sand on the seashore. Because of faith also Sarah herself received physical power to conceive a child, even when she was long past the age for it, because she considered God who had given her the promise to be reliable and trustworthy and true to His word."
—Hebrews 11:11-12

I Do Not Have To Understand The Journey To Trust It.

Creating In Love

Date: Mood: Days Till Ovulation:

I Started My Day Believing: | Last Night I Slept:

My Body Is: | Did I Attempt To Conceive Last Night
                                         | Or Anytime Today?

Today God Told Me: | The Position I Attempted To
                                         | Conceive In:

Today I Envisioned Myself: | Did I Orgasm?

Today's Milestone: | Basal Body Temperature:

Today I Ate: | Cevical Mucus Changes:

Medications And Supplements I Took | Emotional Changes I Have Noticed
Today: | Within Myself:

Did I Take A Pregnancy Test Today? Highlight Yes Or No.

If Yes, What Were The Results? _____.

Creating In Love

Date: Mood: Days Till Ovulation:

I Started My Day Believing: Last Night I Slept:

My Body Is: Did I Attempt To Conceive Last Night Or Anytime Today?

Today God Told Me: The Position I Attempted To Conceive In:

Today I Envisioned Myself: Did I Orgasm?

Today's Milestone: Basal Body Temperature:

Today I Ate: Cevical Mucus Changes:

Medications And Supplements I Took Today: Emotional Changes I Have Noticed Within Myself:

Did I Take A Pregnancy Test Today? Highlight Yes Or No.

If Yes, What Were The Results? _____.

Creating In Love

Date: Mood: Days Till Ovulation:

I Started My Day Believing: Last Night I Slept:

My Body Is: Did I Attempt To Conceive Last Night Or Anytime Today?

Today God Told Me: The Position I Attempted To Conceive In:

Today I Envisioned Myself: Did I Orgasm?

Today's Milestone: Basal Body Temperature:

Today I Ate: Cevical Mucus Changes:

Medications And Supplements I Took Today: Emotional Changes I Have Noticed Within Myself:

Did I Take A Pregnancy Test Today? Highlight Yes Or No.

If Yes, What Were The Results? _____.

My Personal Thoughts

Creating In Love

Date: Mood: Days Till Ovulation:

I Started My Day Believing: Last Night I Slept:

My Body Is: Did I Attempt To Conceive Last Night
                                         Or Anytime Today?

Today God Told Me: The Position I Attempted To
                                         Conceive In:

Today I Envisioned Myself: Did I Orgasm?

Today's Milestone: Basal Body Temperature:

Today I Ate: Cevical Mucus Changes:

Medications And Supplements I Took   Emotional Changes I Have Noticed
Today: Within Myself:

Did I Take A Pregnancy Test Today? Highlight Yes Or No.

If Yes, What Were The Results? _____.

Creating In Love

Date: Mood: Days Till Ovulation:

I Started My Day Believing: Last Night I Slept:

My Body Is: Did I Attempt To Conceive Last Night Or Anytime Today?

Today God Told Me: The Position I Attempted To Conceive In:

Today I Envisioned Myself: Did I Orgasm?

Today's Milestone: Basal Body Temperature:

Today I Ate: Cevical Mucus Changes:

Medications And Supplements I Took Today: Emotional Changes I Have Noticed Within Myself:

Did I Take A Pregnancy Test Today? Highlight Yes Or No.

If Yes, What Were The Results? _____.

Creating In Love

Date: Mood: Days Till Ovulation:

I Started My Day Believing: Last Night I Slept:

My Body Is: Did I Attempt To Conceive Last Night
                         Or Anytime Today?

Today God Told Me: The Position I Attempted To
                                Conceive In:

Today I Envisioned Myself: Did I Orgasm?

Today's Milestone: Basal Body Temperature:

Today I Ate: Cevical Mucus Changes:

Medications And Supplements I Took   Emotional Changes I Have Noticed
Today: Within Myself:

Did I Take A Pregnancy Test Today? Highlight Yes Or No.

If Yes, What Were The Results? _____.

Creating In Love

Date: Mood: Days Till Ovulation:

I Started My Day Believing:

Last Night I Slept:

My Body Is:

Did I Attempt To Conceive Last Night Or Anytime Today?

Today God Told Me:

The Position I Attempted To Conceive In:

Today I Envisioned Myself:

Did I Orgasm?

Today's Milestone:

Basal Body Temperature:

Today I Ate:

Cevical Mucus Changes:

Medications And Supplements I Took Today:

Emotional Changes I Have Noticed Within Myself:

Did I Take A Pregnancy Test Today? Highlight Yes Or No.

If Yes, What Were The Results? _____.

My Life Is In Perfect Balance.

It May Not
Of Happened
This Time
But It Will
Happen At The
Right Time.

Creating In Love

Date: Mood: Days Till Ovulation:

I Started My Day Believing:

Last Night I Slept:

My Body Is:

Did I Attempt To Conceive Last Night Or Anytime Today?

Today God Told Me:

The Position I Attempted To Conceive In:

Today I Envisioned Myself:

Did I Orgasm?

Today's Milestone:

Basal Body Temperature:

Today I Ate:

Cevical Mucus Changes:

Medications And Supplements I Took Today:

Emotional Changes I Have Noticed Within Myself:

Did I Take A Pregnancy Test Today? Highlight Yes Or No.

If Yes, What Were The Results? _____.

Creating In Love

Date: Mood: Days Till Ovulation:

I Started My Day Believing: | Last Night I Slept:

My Body Is: | Did I Attempt To Conceive Last Night Or Anytime Today?

Today God Told Me: | The Position I Attempted To Conceive In:

Today I Envisioned Myself: | Did I Orgasm?

Today's Milestone: | Basal Body Temperature:

Today I Ate: | Cevical Mucus Changes:

Medications And Supplements I Took Today: | Emotional Changes I Have Noticed Within Myself:

Did I Take A Pregnancy Test Today? Highlight Yes Or No.

If Yes, What Were The Results? _____.

Creating In Love

Date: Mood: Days Till Ovulation:

I Started My Day Believing: Last Night I Slept:

My Body Is: Did I Attempt To Conceive Last Night
                                     Or Anytime Today?

Today God Told Me: The Position I Attempted To
                                     Conceive In:

Today I Envisioned Myself: Did I Orgasm?

Today's Milestone: Basal Body Temperature:

Today I Ate: Cevical Mucus Changes:

Medications And Supplements I Took   Emotional Changes I Have Noticed
Today: Within Myself:

Did I Take A Pregnancy Test Today? Highlight Yes Or No.

If Yes, What Were The Results? _____.

My Personal Thoughts

My Ideal Baby Shower Will Look And Feel....

Creating In Love

Date: Mood: Days Till Ovulation:

I Started My Day Believing: Last Night I Slept:

My Body Is: Did I Attempt To Conceive Last Night
                                       Or Anytime Today?

Today God Told Me: The Position I Attempted To
                                       Conceive In:

Today I Envisioned Myself: Did I Orgasm?

Today's Milestone: Basal Body Temperature:

Today I Ate: Cevical Mucus Changes:

Medications And Supplements I Took   Emotional Changes I Have Noticed
Today: Within Myself:

Did I Take A Pregnancy Test Today? Highlight Yes Or No.

If Yes, What Were The Results? _____.

Creating In Love

Date: Mood: Days Till Ovulation:

I Started My Day Believing: Last Night I Slept:

My Body Is: Did I Attempt To Conceive Last Night
                                       Or Anytime Today?

Today God Told Me: The Position I Attempted To
                                       Conceive In:

Today I Envisioned Myself: Did I Orgasm?

Today's Milestone: Basal Body Temperature:

Today I Ate: Cevical Mucus Changes:

Medications And Supplements I Took   Emotional Changes I Have Noticed
Today: Within Myself:

Did I Take A Pregnancy Test Today? Highlight Yes Or No.

If Yes, What Were The Results? _____.

I Am Visualizing The Color Of Love Surrounding Me At This Moment.

223

Creating In Love

Date: Mood: Days Till Ovulation:

I Started My Day Believing: Last Night I Slept:

My Body Is: Did I Attempt To Conceive Last Night
                                                            Or Anytime Today?

Today God Told Me: The Position I Attempted To
                                                            Conceive In:

Today I Envisioned Myself: Did I Orgasm?

Today's Milestone: Basal Body Temperature:

Today I Ate: Cevical Mucus Changes:

Medications And Supplements I Took   Emotional Changes I Have Noticed
Today: Within Myself:

Did I Take A Pregnancy Test Today? Highlight Yes Or No.

If Yes, What Were The Results? _____.

Creating In Love

Date: Mood: Days Till Ovulation:

I Started My Day Believing: Last Night I Slept:

My Body Is: Did I Attempt To Conceive Last Night Or Anytime Today?

Today God Told Me: The Position I Attempted To Conceive In:

Today I Envisioned Myself: Did I Orgasm?

Today's Milestone: Basal Body Temperature:

Today I Ate: Cevical Mucus Changes:

Medications And Supplements I Took Today: Emotional Changes I Have Noticed Within Myself:

Did I Take A Pregnancy Test Today? Highlight Yes Or No.

If Yes, What Were The Results? _____.

Creating In Love

Date: Mood: Days Till Ovulation:

I Started My Day Believing: Last Night I Slept:

My Body Is: Did I Attempt To Conceive Last Night
                                         Or Anytime Today?

Today God Told Me: The Position I Attempted To
                                         Conceive In:

Today I Envisioned Myself: Did I Orgasm?

Today's Milestone: Basal Body Temperature:

Today I Ate: Cevical Mucus Changes:

Medications And Supplements I Took   Emotional Changes I Have Noticed
Today: Within Myself:

Did I Take A Pregnancy Test Today? Highlight Yes Or No.

If Yes, What Were The Results? _____.

There Is
A Reason
Why I
Must Wait
And Still
Try.

This Is Just A Part Of The Story.

Creating In Love

Date: Mood: Days Till Ovulation:

I Started My Day Believing: | Last Night I Slept:

My Body Is: | Did I Attempt To Conceive Last Night Or Anytime Today?

Today God Told Me: | The Position I Attempted To Conceive In:

Today I Envisioned Myself: | Did I Orgasm?

Today's Milestone: | Basal Body Temperature:

Today I Ate: | Cevical Mucus Changes:

Medications And Supplements I Took Today: | Emotional Changes I Have Noticed Within Myself:

Did I Take A Pregnancy Test Today? Highlight Yes Or No.

If Yes, What Were The Results? _____.

Creating In Love

Date: Mood: Days Till Ovulation:

I Started My Day Believing: Last Night I Slept:

My Body Is: Did I Attempt To Conceive Last Night
                                     Or Anytime Today?

Today God Told Me: The Position I Attempted To
                                     Conceive In:

Today I Envisioned Myself: Did I Orgasm?

Today's Milestone: Basal Body Temperature:

Today I Ate: Cevical Mucus Changes:

Medications And Supplements I Took   Emotional Changes I Have Noticed
Today: Within Myself:

Did I Take A Pregnancy Test Today? Highlight Yes Or No.

If Yes, What Were The Results? _____.

Creating In Love

Date: Mood: Days Till Ovulation:

I Started My Day Believing: Last Night I Slept:

My Body Is: Did I Attempt To Conceive Last Night
                                     Or Anytime Today?

Today God Told Me: The Position I Attempted To
                                     Conceive In:

Today I Envisioned Myself: Did I Orgasm?

Today's Milestone: Basal Body Temperature:

Today I Ate: Cevical Mucus Changes:

Medications And Supplements I Took   Emotional Changes I Have Noticed
Today: Within Myself:

Did I Take A Pregnancy Test Today? Highlight Yes Or No.

If Yes, What Were The Results? _____.

My Personal Thoughts

Creating In Love

Date: Mood: Days Till Ovulation:

I Started My Day Believing: Last Night I Slept:

My Body Is: Did I Attempt To Conceive Last Night
                                     Or Anytime Today?

Today God Told Me: The Position I Attempted To
                                     Conceive In:

Today I Envisioned Myself: Did I Orgasm?

Today's Milestone: Basal Body Temperature:

Today I Ate: Cevical Mucus Changes:

Medications And Supplements I Took   Emotional Changes I Have Noticed
Today: Within Myself:

Did I Take A Pregnancy Test Today? Highlight Yes Or No.

If Yes, What Were The Results? _____.

Creating In Love

Date: Mood: Days Till Ovulation:

I Started My Day Believing: Last Night I Slept:

My Body Is: Did I Attempt To Conceive Last Night
                                     Or Anytime Today?

Today God Told Me: The Position I Attempted To
                                     Conceive In:

Today I Envisioned Myself: Did I Orgasm?

Today's Milestone: Basal Body Temperature:

Today I Ate: Cevical Mucus Changes:

Medications And Supplements I Took   Emotional Changes I Have Noticed
Today: Within Myself:

Did I Take A Pregnancy Test Today? Highlight Yes Or No.

If Yes, What Were The Results? _____.

Creating In Love

Date: Mood: Days Till Ovulation:

I Started My Day Believing: Last Night I Slept:

My Body Is: Did I Attempt To Conceive Last Night Or Anytime Today?

Today God Told Me: The Position I Attempted To Conceive In:

Today I Envisioned Myself: Did I Orgasm?

Today's Milestone: Basal Body Temperature:

Today I Ate: Cevical Mucus Changes:

Medications And Supplements I Took Today: Emotional Changes I Have Noticed Within Myself:

Did I Take A Pregnancy Test Today? Highlight Yes Or No.

If Yes, What Were The Results? _____.

Creating In Love

Date: Mood: Days Till Ovulation:

I Started My Day Believing: Last Night I Slept:

My Body Is: Did I Attempt To Conceive Last Night
                                     Or Anytime Today?

Today God Told Me: The Position I Attempted To
                                     Conceive In:

Today I Envisioned Myself: Did I Orgasm?

Today's Milestone: Basal Body Temperature:

Today I Ate: Cevical Mucus Changes:

Medications And Supplements I Took   Emotional Changes I Have Noticed
Today: Within Myself:

Did I Take A Pregnancy Test Today? Highlight Yes Or No.

If Yes, What Were The Results? _____.

I Have Released These Thoughts....

Creating In Love

Date: Mood: Days Till Ovulation:

I Started My Day Believing: Last Night I Slept:

My Body Is: Did I Attempt To Conceive Last Night Or Anytime Today?

Today God Told Me: The Position I Attempted To Conceive In:

Today I Envisioned Myself: Did I Orgasm?

Today's Milestone: Basal Body Temperature:

Today I Ate: Cevical Mucus Changes:

Medications And Supplements I Took Today: Emotional Changes I Have Noticed Within Myself:

Did I Take A Pregnancy Test Today? Highlight Yes Or No.

If Yes, What Were The Results? _____.

Creating In Love

Date: Mood: Days Till Ovulation:

I Started My Day Believing: Last Night I Slept:

My Body Is: Did I Attempt To Conceive Last Night Or Anytime Today?

Today God Told Me: The Position I Attempted To Conceive In:

Today I Envisioned Myself: Did I Orgasm?

Today's Milestone: Basal Body Temperature:

Today I Ate: Cevical Mucus Changes:

Medications And Supplements I Took Today: Emotional Changes I Have Noticed Within Myself:

Did I Take A Pregnancy Test Today? Highlight Yes Or No.

If Yes, What Were The Results? _____.

My Personal Thoughts

Creating In Love

Date: Mood: Days Till Ovulation:

I Started My Day Believing: Last Night I Slept:

My Body Is: Did I Attempt To Conceive Last Night
                                     Or Anytime Today?

Today God Told Me: The Position I Attempted To
                                     Conceive In:

Today I Envisioned Myself: Did I Orgasm?

Today's Milestone: Basal Body Temperature:

Today I Ate: Cevical Mucus Changes:

Medications And Supplements I Took   Emotional Changes I Have Noticed
Today: Within Myself:

Did I Take A Pregnancy Test Today? Highlight Yes Or No.

If Yes, What Were The Results? _____.

My Body Is Nourishing The Child Within Me.

241

Creating In Love

Date: Mood: Days Till Ovulation:

I Started My Day Believing: Last Night I Slept:

My Body Is: Did I Attempt To Conceive Last Night Or Anytime Today?

Today God Told Me: The Position I Attempted To Conceive In:

Today I Envisioned Myself: Did I Orgasm?

Today's Milestone: Basal Body Temperature:

Today I Ate: Cevical Mucus Changes:

Medications And Supplements I Took Today: Emotional Changes I Have Noticed Within Myself:

Did I Take A Pregnancy Test Today? Highlight Yes Or No.

If Yes, What Were The Results? _____.

Creating In Love

Date: Mood: Days Till Ovulation:

I Started My Day Believing: Last Night I Slept:

My Body Is: Did I Attempt To Conceive Last Night
                                     Or Anytime Today?

Today God Told Me: The Position I Attempted To
                                     Conceive In:

Today I Envisioned Myself: Did I Orgasm?

Today's Milestone: Basal Body Temperature:

Today I Ate: Cevical Mucus Changes:

Medications And Supplements I Took   Emotional Changes I Have Noticed
Today: Within Myself:

Did I Take A Pregnancy Test Today? Highlight Yes Or No.

If Yes, What Were The Results? _____.

Creating In Love

I Am Grateful For All That I Am And Everything That I Have.

Date: Mood: Days Till Ovulation:

I Started My Day Believing: Last Night I Slept:

My Body Is: Did I Attempt To Conceive Last Night Or Anytime Today?

Today God Told Me: The Position I Attempted To Conceive In:

Today I Envisioned Myself: Did I Orgasm?

Today's Milestone: Basal Body Temperature:

Today I Ate: Cevical Mucus Changes:

Medications And Supplements I Took Today: Emotional Changes I Have Noticed Within Myself:

Did I Take A Pregnancy Test Today? Highlight Yes Or No.

If Yes, What Were The Results? _____.

I Will Not Let Anyone's No Trumph God's Yes In My Life.

Creating In Love

Date: Mood: Days Till Ovulation:

I Started My Day Believing: Last Night I Slept:

My Body Is: Did I Attempt To Conceive Last Night Or Anytime Today?

Today God Told Me: The Position I Attempted To Conceive In:

Today I Envisioned Myself: Did I Orgasm?

Today's Milestone: Basal Body Temperature:

Today I Ate: Cevical Mucus Changes:

Medications And Supplements I Took Today: Emotional Changes I Have Noticed Within Myself:

Did I Take A Pregnancy Test Today? Highlight Yes Or No.

If Yes, What Were The Results? _____.

Creating In Love

Date: Mood: Days Till Ovulation:

I Started My Day Believing: Last Night I Slept:

My Body Is: Did I Attempt To Conceive Last Night Or Anytime Today?

Today God Told Me: The Position I Attempted To Conceive In:

Today I Envisioned Myself: Did I Orgasm?

Today's Milestone: Basal Body Temperature:

Today I Ate: Cevical Mucus Changes:

Medications And Supplements I Took Today: Emotional Changes I Have Noticed Within Myself:

Did I Take A Pregnancy Test Today? Highlight Yes Or No.

If Yes, What Were The Results? _____.

I Have Faith That Everything Will Work Out.

Creating In Love

Date: Mood: Days Till Ovulation:

I Started My Day Believing: Last Night I Slept:

My Body Is: Did I Attempt To Conceive Last Night Or Anytime Today?

Today God Told Me: The Position I Attempted To Conceive In:

Today I Envisioned Myself: Did I Orgasm?

Today's Milestone: Basal Body Temperature:

Today I Ate: Cevical Mucus Changes:

Medications And Supplements I Took Today: Emotional Changes I Have Noticed Within Myself:

Did I Take A Pregnancy Test Today? Highlight Yes Or No.

If Yes, What Were The Results? _____.

Creating In Love

Date: Mood: Days Till Ovulation:

I Started My Day Believing: Last Night I Slept:

My Body Is: Did I Attempt To Conceive Last Night Or Anytime Today?

Today God Told Me: The Position I Attempted To Conceive In:

Today I Envisioned Myself: Did I Orgasm?

Today's Milestone: Basal Body Temperature:

Today I Ate: Cevical Mucus Changes:

Medications And Supplements I Took Today: Emotional Changes I Have Noticed Within Myself:

Did I Take A Pregnancy Test Today? Highlight Yes Or No.

If Yes, What Were The Results? _____.

I Will Support My Child With Everything That I Have.

Faith In God Includes Faith In His Timing.

I Choose To Let Go And Have Fun During This Process.

Creating In Love

Date: Mood: Days Till Ovulation:

I Started My Day Believing: Last Night I Slept:

My Body Is: Did I Attempt To Conceive Last Night Or Anytime Today?

Today God Told Me: The Position I Attempted To Conceive In:

Today I Envisioned Myself: Did I Orgasm?

Today's Milestone: Basal Body Temperature:

Today I Ate: Cevical Mucus Changes:

Medications And Supplements I Took Today: Emotional Changes I Have Noticed Within Myself:

Did I Take A Pregnancy Test Today? Highlight Yes Or No.

If Yes, What Were The Results? _____.

Creating In Love

Date: Mood: Days Till Ovulation:

I Started My Day Believing: Last Night I Slept:

My Body Is: Did I Attempt To Conceive Last Night
                                       Or Anytime Today?

Today God Told Me: The Position I Attempted To
                                       Conceive In:

Today I Envisioned Myself: Did I Orgasm?

Today's Milestone: Basal Body Temperature:

Today I Ate: Cevical Mucus Changes:

Medications And Supplements I Took   Emotional Changes I Have Noticed
Today: Within Myself:

Did I Take A Pregnancy Test Today? Highlight Yes Or No.

If Yes, What Were The Results? _____.

I Enjoy Life And Everything It Has To Offer Me To The Fullest.

Creating In Love

Date: Mood: Days Till Ovulation:

I Started My Day Believing: Last Night I Slept:

My Body Is: Did I Attempt To Conceive Last Night Or Anytime Today?

Today God Told Me: The Position I Attempted To Conceive In:

Today I Envisioned Myself: Did I Orgasm?

Today's Milestone: Basal Body Temperature:

Today I Ate: Cevical Mucus Changes:

Medications And Supplements I Took Today: Emotional Changes I Have Noticed Within Myself:

Did I Take A Pregnancy Test Today? Highlight Yes Or No.

If Yes, What Were The Results? _____.

Then God remembered Rachel; he listened to her and enabled her To conceive.

– Genesis 30:22

Creating In Love

Date: Mood: Days Till Ovulation:

I Started My Day Believing: Last Night I Slept:

My Body Is: Did I Attempt To Conceive Last Night
                                     Or Anytime Today?

Today God Told Me: The Position I Attempted To
                                     Conceive In:

Today I Envisioned Myself: Did I Orgasm?

Today's Milestone: Basal Body Temperature:

Today I Ate: Cevical Mucus Changes:

Medications And Supplements I Took   Emotional Changes I Have Noticed
Today: Within Myself:

Did I Take A Pregnancy Test Today? Highlight Yes Or No.

If Yes, What Were The Results? _____.

Creating In Love

Date: Mood: Days Till Ovulation:

I Started My Day Believing:	Last Night I Slept:
My Body Is:	Did I Attempt To Conceive Last Night Or Anytime Today?
Today God Told Me:	The Position I Attempted To Conceive In:
Today I Envisioned Myself:	Did I Orgasm?
Today's Milestone:	Basal Body Temperature:
Today I Ate:	Cevical Mucus Changes:
Medications And Supplements I Took Today:	Emotional Changes I Have Noticed Within Myself:

Did I Take A Pregnancy Test Today? Highlight Yes Or No.

If Yes, What Were The Results? _____.

I Know I Will Be A Good Mother To A Happy And Healthy Child.

Creating In Love

Date: Mood:

Days Till Ovulation:

I Started My Day Believing:

Last Night I Slept:

My Body Is:

Did I Attempt To Conceive Last Night Or Anytime Today?

Today God Told Me:

The Position I Attempted To Conceive In:

Today I Envisioned Myself:

Did I Orgasm?

Today's Milestone:

Basal Body Temperature:

Today I Ate:

Cevical Mucus Changes:

Medications And Supplements I Took Today:

Emotional Changes I Have Noticed Within Myself:

Did I Take A Pregnancy Test Today? Highlight Yes Or No.

If Yes, What Were The Results? _____.

My Body Is Ready To Carry Life.

Always Thinking Positive.

I Have The Heart Of A Great Mother.

Creating In Love

Date: Mood: Days Till Ovulation:

I Started My Day Believing: Last Night I Slept:

My Body Is: Did I Attempt To Conceive Last Night Or Anytime Today?

Today God Told Me: The Position I Attempted To Conceive In:

Today I Envisioned Myself: Did I Orgasm?

Today's Milestone: Basal Body Temperature:

Today I Ate: Cevical Mucus Changes:

Medications And Supplements I Took Today: Emotional Changes I Have Noticed Within Myself:

Did I Take A Pregnancy Test Today? Highlight Yes Or No.

If Yes, What Were The Results? _____.

Creating In Love

Date: _____ Mood: _____ Days Till Ovulation: _____

I Started My Day Believing:	Last Night I Slept:
My Body Is:	Did I Attempt To Conceive Last Night Or Anytime Today?
Today God Told Me:	The Position I Attempted To Conceive In:
Today I Envisioned Myself:	Did I Orgasm?
Today's Milestone:	Basal Body Temperature:
Today I Ate:	Cevical Mucus Changes:
Medications And Supplements I Took Today:	Emotional Changes I Have Noticed Within Myself:

Did I Take A Pregnancy Test Today? Highlight Yes Or No.

If Yes, What Were The Results? _____.

I Am In Love With My Pregnant Body.

Creating In Love

Date: Mood: Days Till Ovulation:

I Started My Day Believing: Last Night I Slept:

My Body Is: Did I Attempt To Conceive Last Night Or Anytime Today?

Today God Told Me: The Position I Attempted To Conceive In:

Today I Envisioned Myself: Did I Orgasm?

Today's Milestone: Basal Body Temperature:

Today I Ate: Cevical Mucus Changes:

Medications And Supplements I Took Today: Emotional Changes I Have Noticed Within Myself:

Did I Take A Pregnancy Test Today? Highlight Yes Or No.

If Yes, What Were The Results? _____.

The Day I Find Out That I Have Conceived, I Will ....

My Personal Thoughts

Creating In Love

Date: _____ Mood: _____ Days Till Ovulation: _____

I Started My Day Believing:	Last Night I Slept:
My Body Is:	Did I Attempt To Conceive Last Night Or Anytime Today?
Today God Told Me:	The Position I Attempted To Conceive In:
Today I Envisioned Myself:	Did I Orgasm?
Today's Milestone:	Basal Body Temperature:
Today I Ate:	Cevical Mucus Changes:
Medications And Supplements I Took Today:	Emotional Changes I Have Noticed Within Myself:

Did I Take A Pregnancy Test Today? Highlight Yes Or No.

If Yes, What Were The Results? _____.

I Feel The Movements Of My Baby Inside Of Me.

Creating In Love

Date: Mood: Days Till Ovulation:

I Started My Day Believing: Last Night I Slept:

My Body Is: Did I Attempt To Conceive Last Night
                                         Or Anytime Today?

Today God Told Me: The Position I Attempted To
                                         Conceive In:

Today I Envisioned Myself: Did I Orgasm?

Today's Milestone: Basal Body Temperature:

Today I Ate: Cevical Mucus Changes:

Medications And Supplements I Took   Emotional Changes I Have Noticed
Today: Within Myself:

Did I Take A Pregnancy Test Today? Highlight Yes Or No.

If Yes, What Were The Results? _____.

Creating In Love

Date: Mood: Days Till Ovulation:

I Started My Day Believing: | Last Night I Slept:

My Body Is: | Did I Attempt To Conceive Last Night Or Anytime Today?

Today God Told Me: | The Position I Attempted To Conceive In:

Today I Envisioned Myself: | Did I Orgasm?

Today's Milestone: | Basal Body Temperature:

Today I Ate: | Cevical Mucus Changes:

Medications And Supplements I Took Today: | Emotional Changes I Have Noticed Within Myself:

Did I Take A Pregnancy Test Today? Highlight Yes Or No.

If Yes, What Were The Results? _____.

People Who Know I Am Trying To Conceive....

People Who Are Praying For Me To Conceive....

I Am Going To Try Again.

Creating In Love

Date: Mood: Days Till Ovulation:

I Started My Day Believing: Last Night I Slept:

My Body Is: Did I Attempt To Conceive Last Night
                                       Or Anytime Today?

Today God Told Me: The Position I Attempted To
                                       Conceive In:

Today I Envisioned Myself: Did I Orgasm?

Today's Milestone: Basal Body Temperature:

Today I Ate: Cevical Mucus Changes:

Medications And Supplements I Took   Emotional Changes I Have Noticed
Today: Within Myself:

Did I Take A Pregnancy Test Today? Highlight Yes Or No.

If Yes, What Were The Results? _____.

Creating In Love

Date: Mood: Days Till Ovulation:

I Started My Day Believing: Last Night I Slept:

My Body Is: Did I Attempt To Conceive Last Night Or Anytime Today?

Today God Told Me: The Position I Attempted To Conceive In:

Today I Envisioned Myself: Did I Orgasm?

Today's Milestone: Basal Body Temperature:

Today I Ate: Cevical Mucus Changes:

Medications And Supplements I Took Today: Emotional Changes I Have Noticed Within Myself:

Did I Take A Pregnancy Test Today? Highlight Yes Or No.

If Yes, What Were The Results? _____.

Creating In Love

Date: Mood: Days Till Ovulation:

I Started My Day Believing: Last Night I Slept:

My Body Is: Did I Attempt To Conceive Last Night Or Anytime Today?

Today God Told Me: The Position I Attempted To Conceive In:

Today I Envisioned Myself: Did I Orgasm?

Today's Milestone: Basal Body Temperature:

Today I Ate: Cevical Mucus Changes:

Medications And Supplements I Took Today: Emotional Changes I Have Noticed Within Myself:

Did I Take A Pregnancy Test Today? Highlight Yes Or No.

If Yes, What Were The Results? _____.

Creating In Love

Date: Mood: Days Till Ovulation:

I Started My Day Believing:	Last Night I Slept:
My Body Is:	Did I Attempt To Conceive Last Night Or Anytime Today?
Today God Told Me:	The Position I Attempted To Conceive In:
Today I Envisioned Myself:	Did I Orgasm?
Today's Milestone:	Basal Body Temperature:
Today I Ate:	Cevical Mucus Changes:
Medications And Supplements I Took Today:	Emotional Changes I Have Noticed Within Myself:

Did I Take A Pregnancy Test Today? Highlight Yes Or No.

If Yes, What Were The Results? _____.

Any Day Now I Will Conceive.

Made in the USA
Columbia, SC
01 November 2019

82328381R00167